CREATIVE DIRECTOR
Christine Ricks

PHOTOGRAPHY TEAM
Mike Brunner, Lauren Dorton, Jennifer Dowling,
Dustin Weant

PATTERN TEAM
Edie McGinnis, Denise Lane, Jessica Woods,
Gregg Allnutt

PROJECT DESIGN TEAM
Jenny Doan, Natalie Earnheart, Janet Yamamoto

EDITOR & COPYWRITERS
Jenny Doan, Natalie Earnheart, Christine Ricks,
Katie Mifsud, Camille Maddox, Nichole Spravzoff,
Edie McGinnis

SEWIST TEAM
Jenny Doan, Natalie Earnheart, Janet Yamamoto,
Carol Henderson, Denise Lane, Janice Richardson,
Jamey Stone

QUILTING & BINDING DEPARTMENT
Sarah Richardson, Betty Bates, Karla Zinkand, Natalie
Loucks, Debbie Elder, Jan Meek, Angela Wilson,
Chelsea White, Mary McPhee, Charlene McCabe,
Dennis Voss, Debbie Allen, Jamee Gilgour, Michelle
Templeton, Frank Jones, Kara Snow, Ethan Lucas,
Devin Ragle, Bruce VanIperen, Lyndia Lovell, Aaron
Crawford, Cyera Cottrill, Deborah Warner, Salena
Smiley, Francesca Flemming, Rachael Joyce, Bernice
Kelly, Deloris Burnett

PRINTING COORDINATORS
Rob Stoebener, Seann Dwyer

PRINTING SERVICES
Walsworth Print Group
803 South Missouri
Marceline, MO 64658

CONTACT US
Missouri Star Quilt Company
114 N Davis
Hamilton, Mo. 64644
888-571-1122
info@missouriquiltco.com

content

2

TWO-WAY STREET 54

WINDMILL 62

PINEAPPLE TABLE RUNNER 70

DRESDEN ZIPPERED POUCH 78

JENNY'S CLASSROOM 86

QUILT TALES 88

Oops! Sometimes we make mistakes.
To find corrections to every issue of Block
go to: www.msqc.co/corrections

hello
from MSQC

As soon as frost begins to form on the front lawn and my breath turns misty in the chilly air, my mind immediately returns to the holiday season. The last issue of the year is always such a fun issue for me as it brings back so many warm memories. It also makes me realize how important it is to spend time with loved ones and how dear those memories become. I adore the preparations and celebrations with family and friends all throughout the month of December. It just makes me smile to see bright, colorful lights everywhere when the days get shorter and to hear Christmas carols on the radio. Whatever this holiday season means for you, I hope you enjoy it thoroughly, surrounded by the people you love.

Sadly, there has been so much tragedy and disaster in the world this year and life as we know it can change in an instant. When disaster strikes, we all want to help, and this year Missouri Star Quilt Co. was able to help gather quilts for people in need. I was amazed and humbled as the quilts began to pour into our warehouse. Close to 8,000 quilts were sent in by kind, thoughtful quilters like you. How amazing! In this wonderful, creative community there are so many doing a great deal of good and I am honored to be a part of it. Never think, "I'm just a quilter," because you can do so much! Thank you for all the time and effort that goes into these projects, but especially, thank you for all the love that you put into them. Thank you for helping so many people. The stitches you make at your sewing machine are changing the world!

JENNY DOAN
MISSOURI STAR QUILT CO

4

TRY OUR APP

It's easy to keep up on every issue of BLOCK magazine. Access it from all your devices. And when you subscribe to BLOCK, it's free with your subscription! For the app search BLOCK magazine in the app store. Available for both Apple and Android.

5

For the tutorial and everything you need to make this quilt visit: www.msqc.co/blockearlywinter17

disappearing hourglass 3

When the winter wind is blowing cold, there is nothing quite like a crackling fire. The scent of the wood is bright and nostalgic, to say nothing of the warmth. Give me a big, cozy quilt and a good book and I could sit by the fire for hours on end. While there is plenty to love about modern life, sometimes the old-fashioned way of life suits me best. Of course, keeping a fire going all winter takes a lot of wood. Thank goodness for my dad and his annual wood cutting tradition.

My parents live on eighty acres of hearty, Midwestern land with rolling hills and hundreds of beautiful trees. Every year as the weather starts to cool, Dad heads out to gather enough firewood to keep the wood stove blazing throughout the winter months. This wood-chopping ritual began years ago, and at eighty-four years of age, Dad's still the one holding the chainsaw.

Dad and my son-in-law, Seth, don their official wood-chopping gear: flannel shirts, jeans, and boots. They stock the big pickup truck with axes, chainsaws, and plenty of hot chocolate, and drive down the path to the trees. Like a pair of handsome lumberjacks, they work from dawn to dusk in the chilly autumn air.

7

Wood burns best when it has had time to dry out—we learned this lesson all too well our first year in Missouri—so Dad always hunts for trees that have fallen and are dead. He uses his powerful chainsaw to cut them down into manageable pieces, and he and Seth load them into the truck, haul them up to the wood barn, and stack them into neat piles.

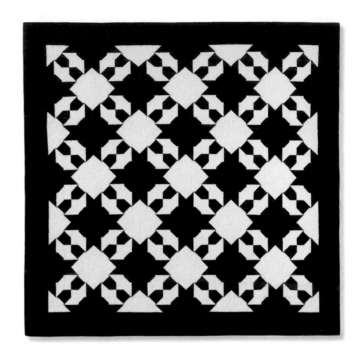

At the end of the day they walk in the door with aching muscles and sawdust in their hair. And like true Midwestern gentlemen, these makeshift lumberjacks don't rest until they have helped the neighbors, too. So for days on end the wood chopping ritual is repeated until every house on the lane is well-stocked with wood for the winter. It's hard work, of course, but nothing compares to the satisfaction of knowing that, come what may, everyone will be warm throughout the winter.

materials

QUILT SIZE
78" x 78" finished

BLOCK SIZE
11¼" finished

QUILT TOP
1 package of 10" background
    squares
1 package of 10" solid squares

OUTER BORDER
1½ yards

BINDING
¾ yard

BACKING
5 yards – vertical seam(s)

SAMPLE QUILT
Bella Solids Black by Moda Fabrics
Bella Solids White by Moda Fabrics

1 sew
make half-square triangles

Layer a 10" background square with a 10" solid square. Sew all the way around the perimeter of the layered squares using a ¼" seam allowance. Cut the sewn square in half twice on the diagonal. Open each half-square triangle and press the seam allowance toward the darker fabric. Each set of sewn squares yields 4 half-square triangle units and 144 are needed. **1A**

1A

10

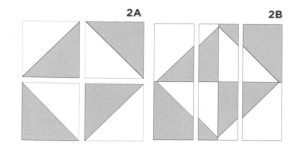

2A   2B

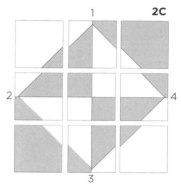

2C

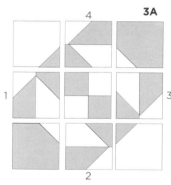

3A

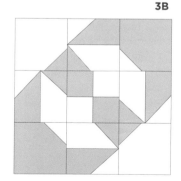

3B

2 block construction

Sew 4 half-square triangle units together into a 4-patch as shown. Square the block to 12¾". 2A

Cut the block into thirds (4¼" sections). If you divide the 4¼" section by 2, you can use the center seam as a guide and simply measure 2⅛" from the center seam and cut vertically on both sides of the seam. 2B

Without moving the pieces, pick up the ruler and measure 2⅛" horizontally from the center seam. Cut on both sides of the center seam. 2C

3 trading places

We are going to be switching and turning some of the segments of the block. The pieces are the outer center of each row. It might make it easier for you to use a numbered pin or a sticky note labeling the pieces. Refer to diagram 3A and notice that piece 1 moved to position 2, 2 moved to position 3, 3 moved to position 4, and 4 moved to position 1. Notice how each piece is oriented. 3A

Sew the pieces back together to make 3 rows of 3 using the new arrangement. Sew the 3 rows together to complete the block. **Make 36.** 3B

Block Size: 11¼" finished

4 arrange and sew

Lay out the blocks in rows. Each row is made up of 6 blocks and 6 rows are needed. Refer to the diagram on page 13 and notice how each block is oriented. After the blocks have been sewn into rows, press the seam allowances of the odd-numbered rows toward the right and the even-numbered rows toward the left to make the seams "nest."

Sew the rows together to complete the center of the quilt.

5 border

Cut (8) 6" strips across the width of the fabric. Sew the strips together end-to-end to make one long strip. Trim the borders from this strip.

Refer to Borders (pg. 103) in the Construction Basics to measure and cut the outer borders. The strips are approximately 67½" for the sides and approximately 78½" for the top and bottom.

6 quilt and bind

Layer the quilt with batting and backing and quilt. After the quilting is complete, square up the quilt and trim away all excess batting and backing. Add binding to complete the quilt. See Construction Basics (pg. 103) for binding instructions.

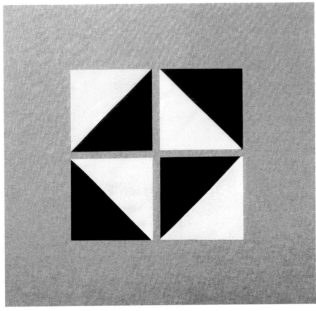

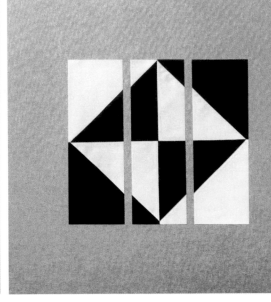

1 Layer a 10" background square with a 10" solid square, with right sides facing. Sew all around the perimeter using a ¼" seam allowance. Cut the sewn square in half twice on the diagonal. Open to reveal 4 half-square triangle units.

2 Sew 4 half-square triangle units together into a 4-patch as shown.

3 After squaring the block to 12¾", measure 2⅛" from the center seam and cut vertically on both sides of the seam.

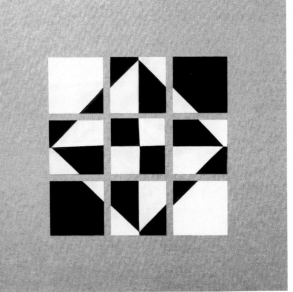

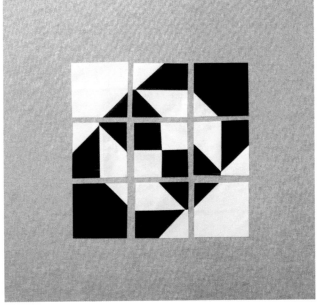

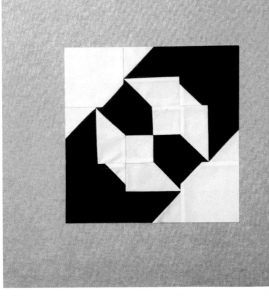

4 Without moving the pieces, pick up the ruler and measure 2⅛" horizontally from the center seam. Cut on both sides of the center seam.

5 Pick up the outer center pieces and move them counterclockwise, thus changing the position and orientation of the pieces as shown.

6 Sew the pieces back together into 3 rows of 3. Sew the rows together to complete the block.

12

dreamweaver

As you may have already gathered, I sure love to sing. I sing when I wake up in the morning, humming to myself as I make my bed. I sing when I'm in the shower and I may even do a little dance too. I especially love to sing when I'm behind the sewing machine. For each and every moment of the day, I can find something to sing about, whether out loud or in my mind. Music is such an important part of my life; I can't imagine going a day without a song.

The great thing about music is, there's so much to choose from. I adore classic musicals, but I'm also up for something with a little more beat. I'm well-versed in a variety of music and there's almost nothing I love more than having a microphone in my hand and an audience listening! Karaoke is at the top of my list for recreational activities, but, sadly, there are no nearby karaoke venues in Hamilton. Well, that just means we have to get a little creative.

For the tutorial and everything
you need to make this quilt visit:
www.msqc.co/blockfall17

On a chilly night there's nothing like gathering around a roaring fire and having a good, old-fashioned Doan family sing-along! Sitting by the fire is one of my favorite pastimes when the winter comes. There's something so soothing about watching the fire and hearing it crackle. And it's especially nice to have my children and grandchildren there with me.

My family has a favorite game we like to play around the fire. We usually split into teams, boys against girls, and play what we simply call "The Song Game." We start by picking a word. It can be any word, let's say the word is "fire." Then

the girls go first and have to come up with a song that has the word fire in it. They have to be able to sing at least one line of a song with the key word in it. Then it's the boys' turn. They all work together to think of a different song using the same word. We go back and forth, singing bits and pieces of songs until no one can think of another song with the keyword and then we pick a new word. We never play this game until someone builds a fire and then it is game on!

Even if you're not the singing type, I hope you get to enjoy some time around a cozy fire this winter. Cuddle up to your loved ones and bask in the warmth, the memories, and the love.

materials

QUILT SIZE
73" x 82"

BLOCK SIZE
8" finished

QUILT TOP
1 roll of 2½" print strips
1¼ yards background fabric
1½ yards sashing - includes inner border
¼ yard for cornerstones

OUTER BORDER
1¼ yards

BINDING
¾ yard

BACKING
5 yards - vertical seam(s)

SAMPLE QUILT
Atelier de France by French General for Moda Fabrics

1 cut

Cut each 2½" strip into (6) 2½" x 4½" rectangles and (6) 2½" squares. Stack all matching pieces together. You need a **total of 224** pieces of each size.

From the background fabric, cut:
- (14) 2½" strips across the width of the fabric. Subcut the strips into 2½" squares. Each strip will yield 16 squares and you need a **total of 224.**

From the sashing fabric, cut:
- (4) 8½" strips across the width of the fabric. Subcut the strips into 1½" x 8½" strips. By cutting the strips vertically, each strip will yield (26) 1½" x 8½" rectangles. You need a **total of 97.** Set the rectangles aside until you have made all of the blocks. The remainder of the fabric will be used for the inner border.

From the fabric you are using for cornerstones, cut:
- (2) 1½" strips across the width of the fabric. Subcut the strips into 1½" squares. Each strip will yield 26 squares and you need a **total of 42.** Set the squares aside until all the blocks are made and you are ready to put the top together.

18

2A

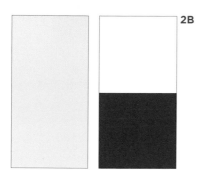

2B

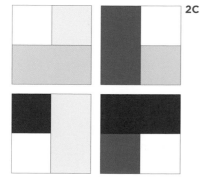

2C

2 block construction

Select a 2½" square and a matching 2½" x 4½" rectangle. You'll need 4 sets to make a complete block. Sew a background 2½" square to a print 2½" square to make a 2½" x 4½" pieced rectangle. **Make 4.** 2A

Sew the 2½" x 4½" pieced rectangle to a 2½" x 4½" rectangle. **Make 4.** 2B

Sew the 4 units together to complete 1 block. Refer to Diagram 2C and notice the way the prints are placed to create the woven look. **Make 56.** 2C

Block size: 8" finished

3 arrange and sew

Lay out the blocks in rows. Each row consists of 7 blocks and you need to make 8 rows. When you are happy with the appearance, begin sewing the rows together, adding a 1½" x 8½" sashing rectangle between each block. Press the sashing strips toward the blocks. 3A

4 make horizontal sashing strips

To one end of a 1½" x 8½" sashing rectangle, sew a 1½" cornerstone. Add another sashing rectangle, then another cornerstone. Continue on in this manner until you have a strip made up of 7 sashing strips and 6 cornerstones.

Press the sashing rectangles toward the cornerstones. **Make 7** sashing strips. 4A

Sew a sashing strip between each row of blocks. Refer to the diagram on page 21, if necessary.

5 inner border

Cut (7) 1½" strips across the width of the fabric. Sew the strips together end-to-end to make one long strip. Trim the borders from this strip.

Refer to Borders (pg. 103) in the Construction Basics to measure and cut the inner borders. The strips are approximately 71½" for the sides and approximately 64½" for the top and bottom.

6 outer border

Cut (8) 5" strips across the width of the fabric. Sew the strips together end-to-end to make one long strip. Trim the borders from this strip.

Refer to Borders (pg. 103) in the Construction Basics to measure and cut the outer borders. The strips are approximately 73½" for the sides and approximately 73½" for the top and bottom.

7 quilt and bind

Layer the quilt with batting and backing and quilt. After the quilting is complete, square up the quilt and trim away all excess batting and backing. Add binding to complete the quilt. See Construction Basics (pg. 103) for binding instructions.

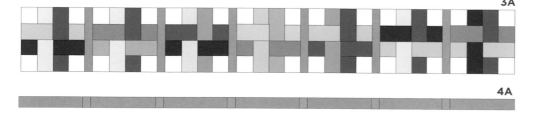

3A

4A

19

1 Select a 2½" square and a matching 2½" x 4½" rectangle. You'll need 4 sets for each block. Sew a 2½" print square to a background 2½" square. Make 4.

2 Add a 2½" x 4½" rectangle to complete one quadrant of the block. Make 4

3 Sew the 4 quadrants together to complete 1 block. Refer to the photo and notice the way the prints are placed to create the woven look.

4 Lay out the blocks in rows and add a sashing rectangle between each block.

5 Make horizontal sashing strips by adding a 1½" cornerstone between each 1½" x 8½" rectangle.

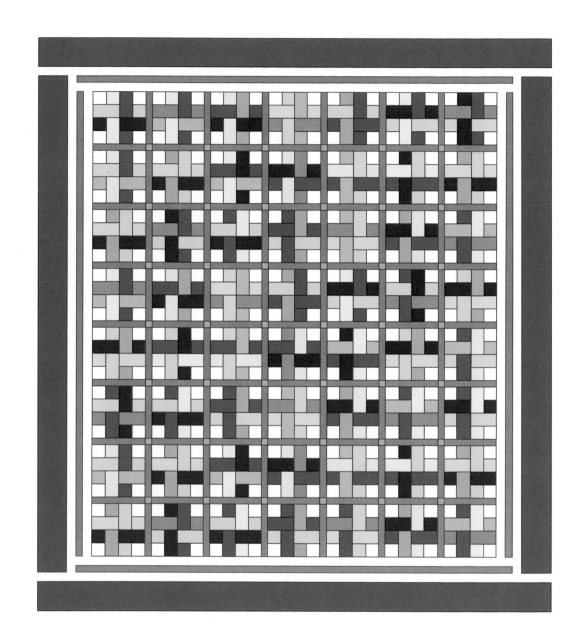

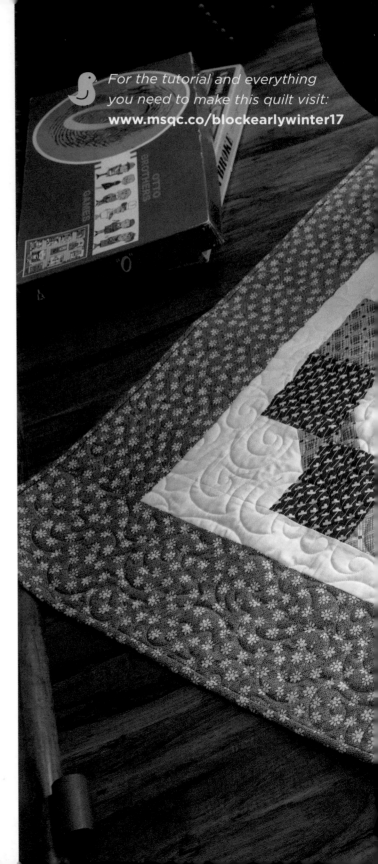

For the tutorial and everything you need to make this quilt visit: **www.msqc.co/blockearlywinter17**

roundabout

New Year's Eve is a magical night filled with fond memories of the year gone by and fresh hopes for the coming year. It's more than just a party, it's a time to celebrate all our small victories and put away past regrets. I love the moment of anticipation when everyone counts down to midnight in unison and rings in the new year. I have been watching the Time Square countdown on TV since I was little, and even now it still gives me a feeling of wonder at the vast gathering of people from all different backgrounds who come together to celebrate. We all have so much to be grateful for and no matter how your year has been, I wish you all the best things in 2018!

This story comes from my friend Ann, who really knows how to celebrate in style. Each year she has a bingo party that everyone raves about!

Bingo isn't the typical game you might play on New Year's Eve, but in our house it's become a family favorite. After the holiday rush, there's nothing like sitting around the dining table, relaxing and spending time together playing a laid-back game of bingo. Each family member brings along a bunch of prizes, usually stocking leftovers and trinkets that have accumulated around the house over the past year, and I make up a few special prizes too—dollar bills folded into cute origami rings—along with plenty of fun-sized candy.

When the game begins, there's always a hushed anticipation that breaks out into friendly chatter once the bingos start popping up. By the end it becomes a competition to see who can reach "blackout" first. Once the game is over and the prizes have all been awarded, it's time for the next activity of the night. And this one isn't quite as tame.

In our family, we like to decorate graham cracker gingerbread houses in the first couple weeks of December, and we enjoy looking at them all month long. But by the end of the month, some of the candy has been picked off by the littles, they're getting stale, and it's time to dispose of them. It seems a shame to dump

them into the trash, so we thought they should get a proper send-off. One year my husband, who's always been young at heart, suggested blowing them up. Along with a modest fireworks display, this tradition is the best part of the night!

When the countdown begins just before midnight and the lawn has been liberally sprinkled with the shrapnel of candy houses, we all gather together and get our noisemakers ready. As the clock strikes twelve, the chaos really begins with horns honking, confetti flying, and hugs and kisses for everyone. There's nothing like it and there's always plenty to clean up afterward, and I wouldn't have it any other way.

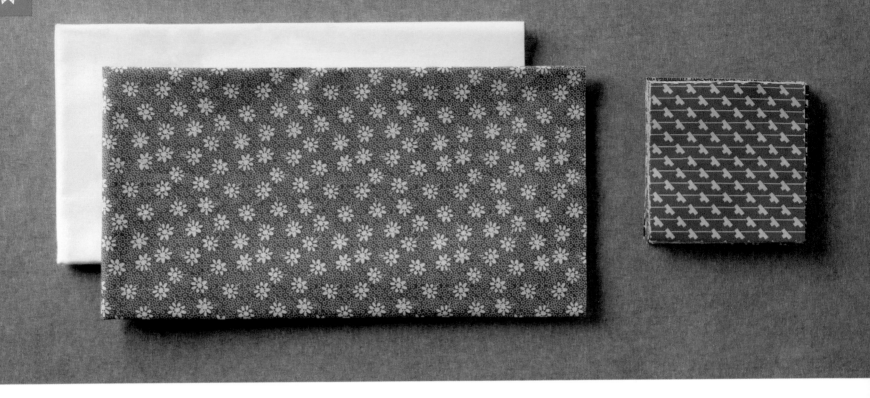

materials

QUILT SIZE
61" X 70"

BLOCK SIZE
9" finished

QUILT TOP
2 packages 5" print squares
1¾ yards background fabric
  – includes inner border

OUTER BORDER
1¼ yards

BINDING
¾ yard

BACKING
4 yards - horizontal seam(s)

SAMPLE QUILT
Sorbet by Leonie Bateman for
Penny Rose Fabrics

1 cut

From the background fabric, cut:

- (8) 5" strips across the width of the fabric—subcut each strip into 5" squares. Each strip will yield 8 squares and a **total of 60** are needed. There will be 4 squares left over for another project.

Set the remainder of the background fabric aside for the inner border.

From the 5" print squares, cut:

- 15 squares in half vertically and horizontally to make 2½" squares. A **total of 60** squares are needed.

2 snowball squares

On the reverse side of each 2½" square, draw a line from corner to corner once on the diagonal. Place a marked square atop a 5" background square with right sides facing. Sew on the marked line, then trim the excess fabric away ¼" from the sewn seam. Press the seam allowance toward the darker fabric.

Make 60. 2A

26

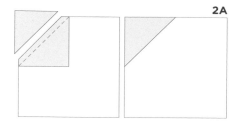

2A

3 block construction

Select 2 matching 5″ squares and 2 snowballed background squares with matching corners. Sew the pieces together in a 4-patch formation as shown. **3A Make 30 blocks.**

Block Size: 9″ finished

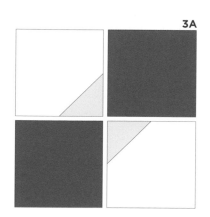

3A

4 arrange and sew

Lay out the blocks in rows with each row made up of 5 blocks. **Make 6 rows**. Refer to the diagram on page 29 for placement.

When you are satisfied with the arrangement, sew the blocks into rows. Press the odd-numbered rows toward the right and the even-numbered rows toward the left to make the seams "nest." Sew the rows together to complete the center of the quilt.

5 inner border

Cut (6) 2½″ strips across the width of the fabric. Sew the strips together end-to-end to make one long strip. Trim the borders from this strip.

Refer to Borders (pg. 103) in the Construction Basics to measure and cut the inner borders. The strips are approximately 54½″ for the sides and approximately 49½″ for the top and bottom.

6 outer border

Cut (6) 6½″ strips across the width of the fabric. Sew the strips together end-to-end to make one long strip. Trim the borders from this strip.

Refer to Borders (pg. 103) in the Construction Basics to measure and cut the outer borders. The strips are approximately 58½″ for the sides and approximately 61½″ for the top and bottom.

7 quilt and bind

Layer the quilt with batting and backing and quilt. After the quilting is complete, square up the quilt and trim away all excess batting and backing. Add binding to complete the quilt. See Construction Basics (pg. 103) for binding instructions.

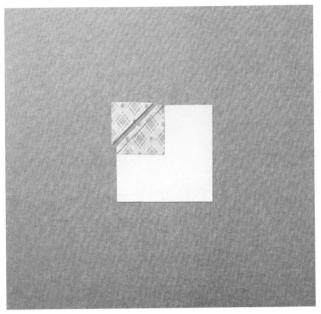

1 Place a marked 2½″ print square atop a 5″ background square with right sides facing. Sew on the marked line, then trim the excess fabric away ¼″ from the sewn seam.

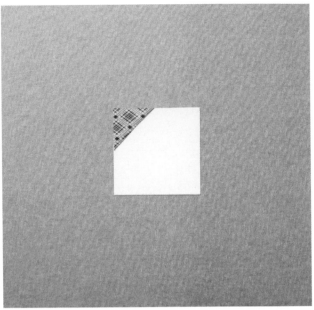

2 Open and press the seam allowance toward the darker fabric.

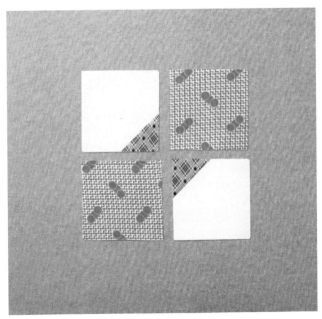

3 Select 2 matching 5″ print squares and 2 snowballed background squares with matching corners. Lay out the pieces in a 4-patch formation.

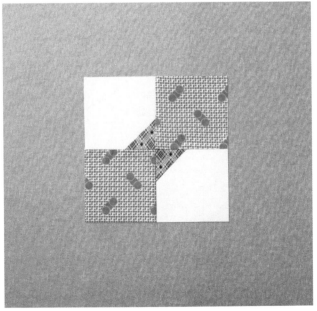

4 Sew the pieces together to complete the block.

sweet blend

It is a rite of passage to host a Thanksgiving dinner. There is so much tradition involved; everything must be just so. After all, everyone expects Aunt Jean's cranberry sauce to be chunky, but not too chunky. The mashed potatoes must be creamy and the gravy smooth. Not to mention the tender yams and moist turkey, the homemade rolls, the green bean casserole, appetizers, decorations, and elaborate place settings. It's a lot to worry about, but timing everything perfectly so it all comes together at exactly 2:00 p.m. is, quite frankly, a magnificent feat.

The year that Margaret decided to take on Thanksgiving, she was nervous but excited. For the first time ever she had invited the family to come. "Don't worry about bringing anything!" She had insisted. "Just come enjoy yourselves. I'll take care of everything."

On Thanksgiving Day, Margaret got up early to make pumpkin pie. When the pies were done, she set them on the counter to cool. Then the turkey was stuffed and placed gently in the oven. Everything was right on schedule, so Margaret took a break to get primped for the day.

For the tutorial and everything you need to make this quilt visit:
www.msqc.co/blockearlywinter17

Minutes later, when she walked back into the kitchen, Margaret was horrified to see the cat leaping down from the counter. Margaret's beautiful pumpkin pies were now decorated with a set of teeny, tiny paw prints. Her heart sank, but in a moment of inspiration, she decided to cover the pies in a thick layer of homemade whipped cream. The pies looked delicious—and no one would know the difference!

The guests began to arrive, but between mashing potatoes and whisking gravy, Margaret didn't have much time to chat. She shooed everyone out of the kitchen. "Go! Relax! Make yourselves at home. Dinner will be ready in no time!" She assured them.

She turned to check on her turkey and, to her horror, the oven was only barely warm. Something was not right! The turkey was a lovely golden brown on the outside, but the center was raw. Margaret tried to crank up the heat, but nothing happened. The oven was dead and the turkey was ruined.

With tears in her eyes, Margaret carried her carefully prepared feast to the table. At exactly 2:00 p.m. the family sat down to their Thanksgiving meal—sans turkey. She felt like a failure, but Margaret soon realized that the meal didn't need to be flawless to be special. The family laughed and told stories, and everyone agreed that the pumpkin pie was especially delicious smothered in whipped cream. In fact, the turkey was hardly missed at all. And that year for Christmas, Margaret treated herself to a brand new, state-of-the-art oven.

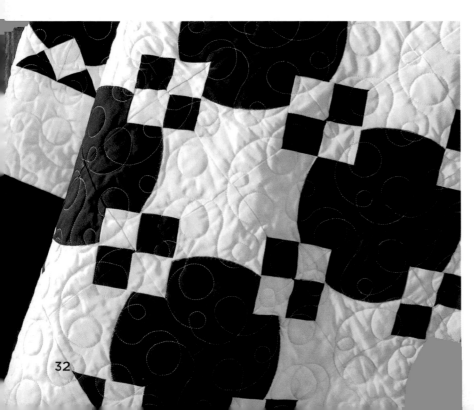

materials

QUILT SIZE
64" X 73"

BLOCK SIZE
9" finished

SUPPLY LIST
3¼ yards dark solid
1 package of 10" background squares
plus 2½ yards **or** 5¼ yards background
fabric - includes borders

BINDING
¾ yard

BACKING
4½ yards - vertical seam(s)

OTHER
Easy Circle Cut Ruler
3¼ yards 24" wide fusible interfacing

SAMPLE QUILT
Kona Cotton Regal Solids by Robert
Kaufman Fabrics
Kona Cotton White Solids by Robert
Kaufman Fabrics

1 cut

From the dark solid fabric, cut:

- (9) 8" strips across the width
  of the fabric – subcut 8 strips
  into (5) 8" squares each. Subcut
  (2) 8" squares from the
  remaining strip.
- (12) 3" strips across the width
  of the fabric – subcut each strip
  into (13) 3" squares for a **total
  of 156**. Cut (12) 3" squares from
  the remainder of the 8" strip.
  Add them to the 156 squares for
  a **total of 168.**

2 background fabric

If you are using precut 10" squares,
skip the cutting directions for the 10"
squares.

If you are using yardage for the
background, cut:

- (11) 10" strips across the width
  of the fabric. Subcut 10 strips
  into (4) 10" squares each for
  a **total of 40 squares.** Subcut
  the remaining strip into (2) 10"
  squares.
- (13) 3" strips across the width of
  the fabric – subcut each strip
  into (13) 3" squares for a **total
  of 168 squares.**

Set the remaining background fabric
aside for the borders.

From the fusible interfacing, cut:

- (14) 8" vertical strips down the
  width of the interfacing – subcut
  each strip into (3) 8" squares for
  a **total of 42.**

34

3 fuse, mark, and cut

Press the fusible interfacing to the reverse side of the 8″ dark solid squares. Turn each square over so the paper side is up. Fold the square in half with right sides facing and place the Easy Circle Cut Ruler on the edge of the fold. Draw a half circle using the 7″ slot.

Note: the cut circle will measure $7\frac{1}{2}″$ because cutting on a particular slot using this ruler makes the unfinished size, thus adding $\frac{1}{2}″$ seam allowance. Cut on the drawn line while the piece is still folded. When the piece is unfolded, you will have a $7\frac{1}{2}″$ circle. **Cut 42 circles.**

Peel off the paper backing from each circle. Center each circle on a 10″ background square.

Note: If you fold the background square in half horizontally and vertically and finger press the creases in place you will be able to center the circle easily. Fuse each circle in place.

When all circles have been fused in place, stitch around each using a small zigzag or blanket stitch.

4 make half-square triangles

Draw a line from corner to corner once on the diagonal on the reverse side of the light 3″ background squares. Layer a marked background square with a dark 3″ square with right sides facing. Sew $\frac{1}{4}″$ on both sides of the line. Cut on the line, open to reveal 2 half-square triangles. Square each half-square triangle to $2\frac{1}{2}″$.

Repeat for the remaining squares to make a **total of 336.** 4A

5 block construction

Cut each fused 10″ square in half vertically and horizontally to make (4) 5″ squares. 5A

Fold a half-square triangle unit once on the diagonal across the seam line and finger press the fold in place. The crease will mark the sewing line. 5B

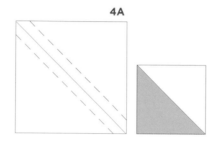

4A

5A

5B

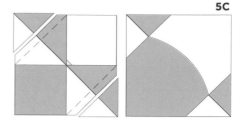

5C

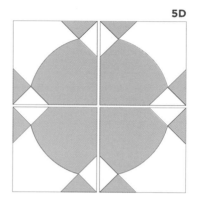

5D

Place a folded half-square triangle on 2 opposing corners of a 5″ square. The background portion of the half-square triangles should touch the dark fused quarter circle. Sew on the creased line. Trim the excess fabric $\frac{1}{4}″$ away from the sewn seam. This makes one quadrant of the block. **Make 4.** 5C

Sew the 4 quadrants together as shown to complete the block. **Make 42.** 5D

Block Size: 9″ finished

6 arrange and sew

Arrange the blocks into rows with each row made up of 6 blocks. **Make 7 rows.** Press the odd-numbered rows toward the right and the even-numbered rows toward the left to make the seams nest easily.

Sew the rows together.

35

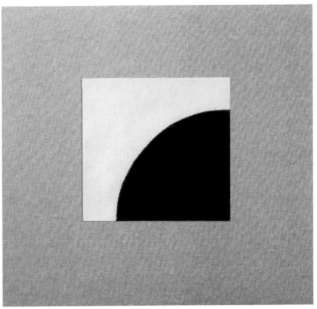

1 Layer a marked 3″ background square with a dark 3″ square with right sides facing. Sew on both sides of the line. Cut on the line, open both sides to reveal 2 half-square triangle units.

2 Cut each fused 10″ square in half vertically and horizontally to make (4) 5″ squares.

3 Fold a half-square triangle unit once on the diagonal across the seam line and finger press the fold in place to mark a sewing line.

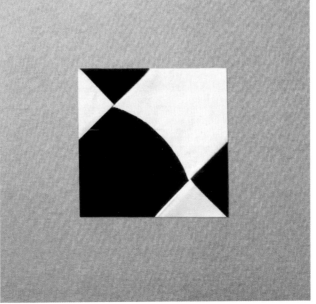

4 Place a folded half-square triangle on 2 opposing corners of a 5″ square. Sew on the creased line. Trim the excess fabric ¼″ away from the sewn seam.

5 Open and press the trimmed unit. This is one quadrant of the block.

6 Sew 4 quadrants together to complete the block.

7 border

Cut (7) 5½" strips across the width of the fabric. Sew the strips together end-to-end to make one long strip. Trim the borders from this strip.

Refer to Borders (pg. 103) in the Construction Basics to measure and cut the outer borders. The strips are approximately 63½" for the sides and approximately 64½" for the top and bottom.

8 quilt and bind

Layer the quilt with batting and backing and quilt. After the quilting is complete, square up the quilt and trim away all excess batting and backing. Add binding to complete the quilt. See Construction Basics (pg. 103) for binding instructions.

stars & pinwheels

There is something magical about the first snow of the season. After a whirlwind summer, the earth finally settles down for a deep, chilly sleep. It comes on slowly at first with a little nip in the morning air, a thin layer of frost sparkling on the front lawn, and culminates with a gaggle of geese thundering across the sky in a flurry of honks and flapping wings. The transformation from summer to fall is slow and gentle, with plenty of warm afternoons thrown in the mix.

Suddenly, after all the fallen leaves have been raked and the Thanksgiving leftovers gobbled up, you pause and realize: it's time for winter! And even though the stores are decked out in tinsel and lights, the dry brown grass outside just doesn't feel very festive. After all, Christmas just isn't Christmas without a thick layer of fluffy, white snow.

If you find yourself wishing for snow this year, you may not have to wait too long. There are a few traditional tricks for getting it to snow that legend says are sure to bring on the storm of the century.

For the tutorial and everything you need to make this quilt visit:
www.msqc.co/blockearlywinter17

Before you go to bed, drop a few ice cubes into the toilet. I recommend one cube for every inch of snow you desire. Don't get too carried away, though, unless you're prepared to dig your way out of a twelve-foot drift!

Place a spoon under your pillow. Why? I have no idea. But I do know that folks have been sleeping on spoons since the time of the pilgrims, and there have been thousands of snowstorms since then. Coincidence? I think not.

Wear your pajamas inside out and backwards. The snow gods will be so confused, you'll see flurries in no time!

Now I'm no snow expert, but these tried-and-true superstitions seem to work remarkably well. In 2014, a group of students in West Haven, Michigan, participated in a county-wide call for snow. Kids of all ages donned inside-out pajamas and slept with spoons under their pillows. They hoped for a storm big enough to cancel school, and whether it was dumb luck or something much more magical, those kids woke up to snow, snow, and more snow! There was so much snow, in fact, school was canceled for two days! I can only imagine the fun that was had building snowmen and sledding down fluffy, white hills.

This year, when you're longing for a white Christmas, I hope you'll give these superstitions a chance—and be sure to let me know if they work! Winter is a wonderful time of year, and it's so much more fun with plenty of beautiful, sparkling snow!

materials

QUILT SIZE
80" x 92"

BLOCK SIZE
12" finished

SUPPLIES
1 package 10" print squares*
5½ yards background fabric
  – includes pieced inner border
*Make sure the print squares you choose
contrast with the background fabric.*

OUTER BORDER
2 yards

BINDING
¾ yard

BACKING
7½ yards - horizontal seam(s)

SAMPLE QUILT
Bloomsbury by Franny & Jane for
Moda Fabrics

1 cut

From the background fabric, cut:

- (72) 2½" strips across the width of the fabric – subcut 51 strips into 2½" x 4½" rectangles. Each strip will yield 8 rectangles and you need a **total of 408**. Set aside 48 rectangles to use in the pieced border. Subcut the remaining (21) 2½" strips into 2½" squares. Each strip will yield 16 squares and you need a **total of 336.** Set aside 96 squares to use in the pieced border.

- (3) 4½" strips across the width of the fabric – subcut each strip into 4½" squares. Each strip will yield 8 squares and you need a **total of 22.** Set aside the squares for the inner pieced border.

From each of (30) 10" squares, cut the following pieces:

- (2) 5" x 10" rectangles – subcut 1 rectangle into (1) 4½" square and (2) 2½" x 4½" rectangles – subcut the remaining rectangle into (8) 2½" squares. Keep all matching 2½" squares together to use when making flying geese A units. You will have a **total of (30)** 4½" squares, **(60)** 2½" x 4½" rectangles and **(240)** 2½" squares.

42

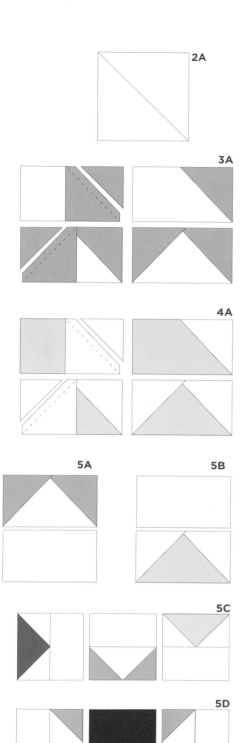

2A

3A

4A

5A   5B

5C

5D

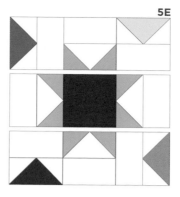

5E

From the remaining 12 squares, cut:
- (2) 4½" x 10" rectangles –
  subcut each rectangle into
  (4) 2½" x 4½" rectangles. Each
  square will yield 8 rectangles.
  You will have a **total of 96
  rectangles.** Stack these with the
  60 rectangles you have already
  cut. You will still need 12 more
  rectangles. We will cut
  those next using the outer
  border fabric.

From the outer border fabric, cut:
- (1) 4½" strip across the width
  of the fabric - subcut the strip
  into 2½" x 4½" rectangles. The
  strip will yield 16 rectangles and
  you need a **total of 12.** Add the
  12 rectangles to the **156** you
  have already cut. Your stack
  should have **168 pieces.** Set
  aside the remaining 4 rectangles
  for another project. Reserve
  the rest of the fabric for the
  outer border.

2 make flying geese
Draw a line from corner to corner once
on the diagonal on the reverse side of

each 2½" square. If you would rather not
take the time to draw the line, just fold
the piece on the diagonal and press a
crease in place to mark a sewing line. **2A**

3 flying geese a
Pick up 8 matching 2½" squares, making
sure the selected squares contrast with
the background fabric. Sew a marked
2½" print square to one end of a 2½"
background strip. Sew on the marked
line, then trim ¼" away from the sewn
seam. Repeat for the other end. **Make 4**
for each block for a **total of 120** flying
geese A units. **3A**

4 flying geese b
Sew a marked 2½" background square
to one end of a 2½" print rectangle. Sew
on the marked line, then trim ¼" away
from the sewn seam. Repeat for the
other end. **Make 4** for each block for a
total of 120 flying geese B units. Set
aside the remaining 2½" x 4½"
print strips to use when making the
pieced inner borders. **4A**

5 block construction
Sew a 2½" x 4½" background rectangle
to a flying geese A unit. **Make 4.** We'll
call these unit A for clarity. **5A**

Sew a 2½" x 4½" background rectangle
to a flying geese B unit. **Make 4.** We'll
call these unit B. **5B**

Sew a unit B to either side of a unit A.
Make 2 rows like this. Be aware of the
way the flying geese are turned. **5C**

43

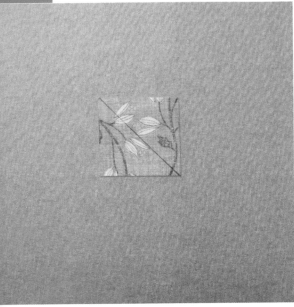

1 Draw a line from corner to corner once on the diagonal on the reverse side of each 2½" square.

2 To make Flying Geese A units, select 8 matching 2½" print squares. Sew a marked 2½" print square to one end of a 2½" background strip. Sew on the marked line, then trim ¼" away from the sewn seam. Repeat for the other end.

3 To make Flying Geese B units, sew a marked 2½" background square to one end of a 2½" print rectangle. Sew on the marked line, then trim ¼" away from the sewn seam. Repeat for the other end.

4 To make unit A, sew a 2½" x 4½" background rectangle to a flying geese A unit.

5 To make unit B, sew a 2½" x 4½" background rectangle to a flying geese B unit.

6 Make the top and bottom row of the block by sewing a unit B to either side of a unit A. Make the center row by sewing a unit A to either side of the center 4½" print square. Sew the 3 rows together to complete the block.

Sew a unit A to either side of the center 4½" print square. **Make 1** row like this. 5D

Sew the 3 rows together as shown to complete 1 block. **Make 30.** 5E

Block Size: 12" finished

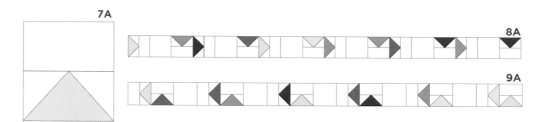

6 arrange and sew

Arrange the blocks into rows. Each row has 5 blocks and 6 rows are needed. When you are pleased with the arrangement, sew the blocks together into rows. Press the odd rows toward the right and the even rows toward the left. This will make the seams "nest."

Sew the rows together to complete the center of the quilt.

7 pieced inner border

Follow the directions on page 43 and **make 48** unit Bs. 7A

8 side borders

Sew a unit B to a 4½" background square. Add a unit B with the flying geese turned toward the top of the strip. Add another unit B with the geese turned toward the outer border. Follow with a background 4½" square. Continue on in this manner until you have a row that begins and ends with a unit B and has (6) 4½" squares. Refer to diagram 8A and **make 2** rows. Sew one to either side of the center of the quilt.

9 top and bottom borders

Begin and end each row with 2 unit Bs. Alternate the unit Bs with a 4½" background square. Refer to diagram 9A and **make 2 rows.** Sew one to the top of the quilt and one to the bottom.

10 outer border

Cut (9) 6½" strips across the width of the fabric. Sew the strips together end-to-end to make one long strip. Trim the borders from this strip.

Refer to Borders (pg. 103) in the Construction Basics to measure and cut the outer borders. The strips are approximately 80½" for the sides and approximately 80½" for the top and bottom.

11 quilt and bind

Layer the quilt with batting and backing and quilt. After the quilting is complete, square up the quilt and trim away all excess batting and backing. Add binding to complete the quilt. See Construction Basics (pg. 103) for binding instructions.

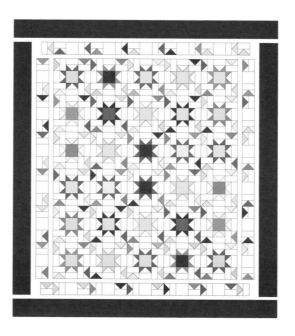

For the tutorial and everything you need to make this quilt visit:
www.msqc.co/blockearlywinter17

take flight

My friend Katie shared this story about her husband Paul. An avid hiker, he has been a Boy Scout leader for most of his life. Although he'd been on many hikes, this one turned out to be different from the rest.

Early in December, Paul and his Boy Scout troop hiked up the winding path to the top of Multnomah Falls. The view from above the falls would be spectacular after a snowfall and the boys were enthusiastic about a change of pace from midwinter knot tying sessions. They wanted to get out in nature and experience the rare sight of snow in Oregon.

The hike began like many others. There were boys who rushed ahead, eager to race to the top while there were others who trailed behind, complaining about the weight of their packs. But Tony and David didn't seem too intent on getting anywhere. They would stop whenever the mood struck them to examine wildlife and explore less-traveled branches of the trail.

As the late afternoon turned to dusk, the Boy Scout troop quickly recognized that they needed to finish their hike before nightfall. They were losing daylight and the trail was difficult to follow beneath the blanket of snow. After taking a headcount, they realized that Tony and David were nowhere to be seen. Retracing their steps, they found them on a side trail, scared, but safe. Unfortunately, the search had cost them valuable time and suddenly it was dark.

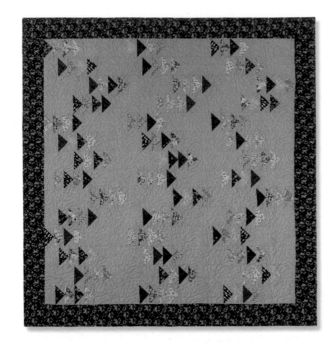

They diverted their hike from the ridge of the gorge and began walking down the side of a slope in a desperate attempt to find the trail. Slipping and sliding on ice, some in tennis shoes, the Scouts scrambled down the hill until they reached a creek at the bottom where they decided to wait for help. They tried to light a fire but were unsuccessful. They huddled around one flashlight and shared the beef jerky and granola bars that were left. One leader stayed with the boys while Paul went for help.

Following the stream, Paul headed down on his own to seek out assistance. He slipped into the stream repeatedly, but after more than three hours he reached the park rangers in Mt. Hood National Forest, wet and exhausted. He was able to pinpoint the location of the Scouts, but the rescuers had a difficult time reaching the boys because the trail was iced over. When the rescuers finally arrived, they quickly lit a fire with one of the boy's Tupperware lunchboxes. After that it wasn't too long before the Scouts were airlifted out of the woods and were headed home again to anxious families.

None of them had imagined that their hike would end in a helicopter ride and they were all grateful to make it home in one piece. Tony and David tearfully promised to never wander off the trail again and were awarded a cowbell for the next hike so everyone would always know where they were. All of the Scouts learned the lesson well to "Always Be Prepared," but most of all, they learned they had a leader who would do everything he could to get them home safely.

48

materials

QUILT SIZE
76½" X 81"

BLOCK SIZE
5" x 10" finished

QUILT TOP
2 packages 5" print squares
3¾ yards background fabric

BORDER
1½ yard

BINDING
¾ yard

BACKING
2 yards 90" wide

SAMPLE QUILT
Indigo Rose by Sara B for Camelot Fabrics

1 cut

From the background fabric, cut:

- (14) 5½" strips across the width of the fabric – subcut each strip into 5½" x 12½" rectangles. Each strip will yield 3 rectangles and a **total of 42** are needed.

- (11) 5" strips across the width of the fabric – subcut each strip into 5" squares. Each strip will yield 8 squares and a **total of 84** are needed.

2A

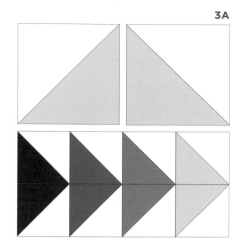

3A

Make 4 and sew them together in a row to complete 1 block. **Make 42**. **3A**

Block Size: 5″ x 10″ finished

4 sew

Beginning with a flying geese block, sew 3 background rectangles and 3 flying geese blocks together, alternating the background pieces with blocks into 1 long strip. **Make 14. 4A**

Sew each row into a loop by stitching the last background rectangle to the first flying geese block.

Cut the loop in two at random intervals between the flying geese blocks to gain a staggered effect.

Lay out the rows and sew them together when you are satisfied with the appearance.

5 border

Cut (8) 6″ strips across the width of the fabric. Sew the strips together end-to-end to make one long strip. Trim the borders from this strip.

Refer to Borders (pg. 103) in the Construction Basics to measure and cut the outer borders. The strips are approximately 70½″ for the sides and approximately 77″ for the top and bottom.

6 quilt and **bind**

Layer the quilt with batting and backing and quilt. After the quilting is complete, square up the quilt and trim away all excess batting and backing. Add binding to complete the quilt. See Construction Basics (pg. 103) for binding instructions.

2 make half-square triangle units

Layer a 5″ background square with a 5″ print square with right sides facing. Sew all the way around the perimeter using a ¼″ seam allowance. Cut the sewn squares from corner to corner twice on the diagonal. Open to reveal 4 half-square triangle units. **Make 336** half-square triangle units and square each to 3″. **2A**

3 block construction

Sew 2 half-square triangles together as shown to make 1 flying geese.

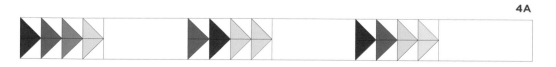

4A

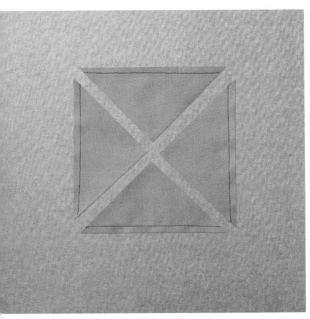

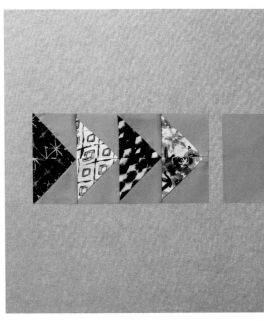

1 Layer a 5″ background square with a 5″ solid square with right sides facing. Sew around the perimeter using a ¼″ seam allowance. Cut the sewn squares from corner to corner twice on the diagonal. Open to reveal 4 half-square triangles. Square each to 3″.

2 Sew 2 matching half-square triangles together to make a flying geese unit.

3 Sew 4 flying geese together to make a block. Alternate 3 flying geese blocks with background rectangles to make a row.

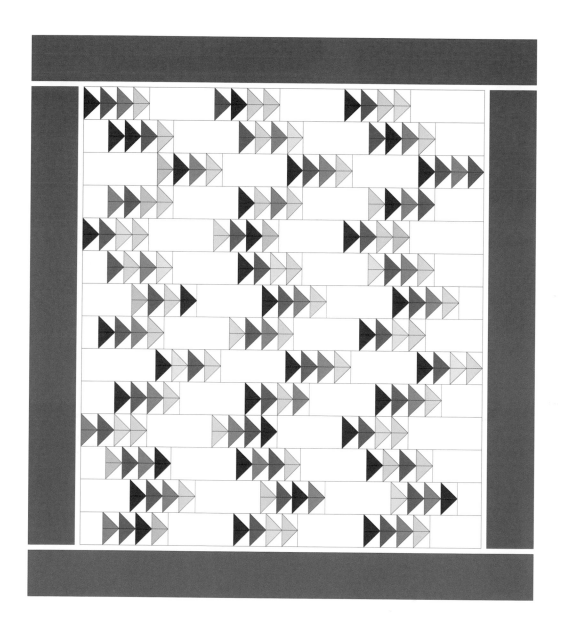

two-way street

Mom always started her Christmas shopping months in advance. She hunted for deals and squirreled away little treasures all year long. By the time Christmas rolled around, the only job left was the wrapping.

In our house, present wrapping was an event all its own. My mother is a master present-wrapper; she believes that even a simple gift feels special when it is wrapped with care. Every package, no matter how large or small, was given special attention, and no two presents could look alike. She had a huge supply of gift wrap and bows: stripes, polka dots, sparkles, and Santas. But that wasn't all. Each wrapped gift was finished off with a special topper. Sometimes it was a small piece of the present, sometimes it was a pretty pinecone, but it was always special and it was always beautiful.

For the tutorial and everything you need to make this quilt visit:
www.msqc.co/blockearlywinter17

55

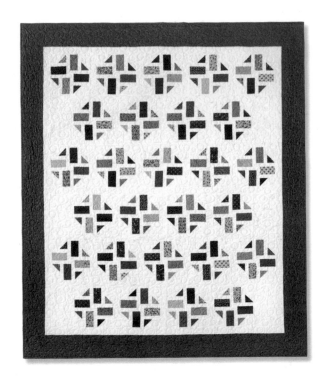

Although it must have tested her patience, Mother did allow us to assist with the wrapping occasionally, but we were expected to do our very best. The paper had to be cut exactly to size. If it was too small, we could never piece it with a scrap—even on the underside. Every crease was folded with care. Tape was placed perfectly straight.

It was an art form—one that took a level of patience and precision that I did not possess. I have always said that finished is better than perfect, and that certainly showed in my wrapping efforts. My corners weren't sharp, but they sure were sturdy—sometimes with extra little wads of paper and plenty of tape.

When I got married and started my own traditions, I quickly figured out that I had married my mother! Ron is a wonderful present wrapper. He takes special care to wrap each little thing, and it is always so much fun to see his beautiful designs, even if they only last until Christmas morning.

If you were to visit this year at Christmas time, you would find beautifully wrapped presents under our tree. Each one is unique and special—a visual representation of our love for each recipient. I am so grateful this tradition has continued, and I'm especially grateful I don't have to do it!

materials

QUILT SIZE
74" x 86"

BLOCK SIZE
10" finished

SUPPLIES
2 packages of 5" print squares
4¼ yards background fabric
– includes inner border

OUTER BORDER
1½ yards

BINDING
¾ yard

BACKING
5¼ yards - vertical seam(s)

SAMPLE QUILT
Oak Grove Lane by Kathy Schmitz
for Moda Fabrics

1 cut

Cut each 5" print square in half to make (2) 2½" x 5" rectangles for a **total of 168**. Subcut 54 of the rectangles into (2) 2½" squares for a **total of 108**.

From the background fabric, cut:

- (4) 5½" strips across the width of the fabric - subcut the strips into 1½" x 5½" rectangles. Each strip will yield 27 rectangles and a **total of 108** are needed.

- (11) 5" strips across the width of the fabric – subcut 7 strips into 2½" x 5" rectangle. Each strip will yield 16 rectangles and a **total of 108** are needed. Subcut the remaining 4 strips into 1½" x 5" rectangles. Each strip will yield 27 rectangles and a **total of 108** are needed.

- (3) 10½" strips across the width of the fabric – subcut 1 strip into (6) 6½" x 10½" rectangles. Set aside to use as setting rectangles. Subcut the remaining 2 strips into 2½" x 10½" rectangles. Each strip will yield 16 and you need a **total of 21**. Set the rectangles aside to use as vertical sashing strips.

58

2A

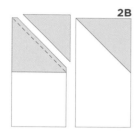

2B

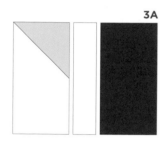

3A

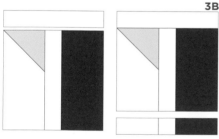

3B

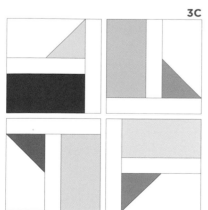

3C

Set the remainder of the background fabric aside for horizontal sashing strips and inner border.

2 snowball rectangles

Mark a sewing line by drawing a line from corner to corner once on the diagonal on the reverse side of each $2\frac{1}{2}$" print square. Or mark the sewing line by pressing a crease in each square once on the diagonal. 2A

Place a marked $2\frac{1}{2}$" square on one end of a $2\frac{1}{2}$" x 5" background rectangle. Sew on the marked line, then trim the excess fabric away $\frac{1}{4}$" from the sewn seam. **Make 108** snowballed rectangles. 2B

3 block construction

Sew a $2\frac{1}{2}$" x 5" print rectangle to a $1\frac{1}{2}$" x 5" background rectangle. Add a snowballed background $2\frac{1}{2}$" x 5" rectangle as shown. 3A

Sew a $1\frac{1}{2}$" x $5\frac{1}{2}$" rectangle to the top of the unit. Square up the unit to $5\frac{1}{2}$" by trimming across the bottom as shown. **Make 4.** 3B

Sew the 4 units together as shown to complete the block. **Make 27.** 3C

Block Size: 10" finished

4 arrange and sew

Lay out the blocks in rows. Rows 1, 3, and 5 are made up of 5 blocks with sashing strips between each block. Rows 2, 4, and 6 are made up of 4 blocks with sashing strips between each block and begin and end with a $6\frac{1}{2}$" x $10\frac{1}{2}$" setting rectangle.

5 make horizontal sashing strips

After the blocks have been sewn into rows, measure several across the width. The rows should average about $58\frac{1}{2}$" across.

Cut (8) $2\frac{1}{2}$" strips across the width of the fabric. Sew the strips together end-to-end and cut the horizontal sashing strips from the length in the same manner as you would cut a border. **Make 5** sashing strips to match your measurement.

Sew the rows together, adding a horizontal sashing strip between each row to complete the center of the quilt.

6 inner border

Cut (7) $2\frac{1}{2}$" strips across the width of the fabric. Sew the strips together end-to-end to make one long strip. Trim the borders from this strip.

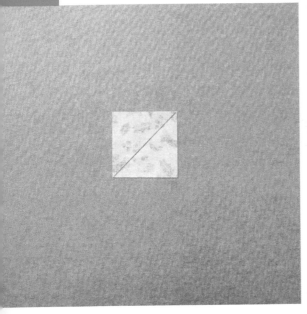

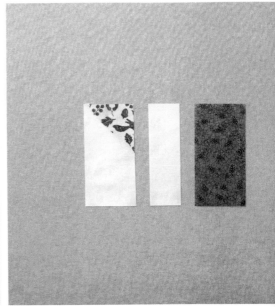

1 Mark a sewing line by drawing a line from corner to corner once on the diagonal on the reverse side of each 2½" print square.

2 Place a marked 2½" square on one end of a 2½" x 5" background rectangle with right sides facing. Sew on the marked line, then trim the excess fabric away ¼" from the sewn seam. Open and press.

3 Sew a 2½" x 5" print rectangle to a 1½" x 5" background rectangle. Add a snowballed background rectangle to the other side as shown.

4 Stitch a 1½" x 5½" rectangle to the top of the unit.

5 Square up the unit to 5½" by trimming across the bottom as shown. Make 4.

6 Lay out 4 units and stitch them together to complete one block.

60

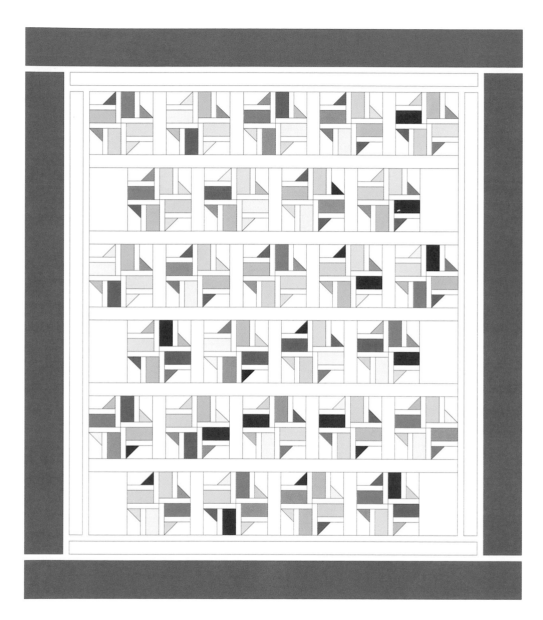

Refer to Borders (pg. 103) in the Construction Basics to measure and cut the inner borders. The strips are approximately 70½" for the sides and approximately 62½" for the top and bottom.

7 outer border

Cut (8) 6½" strips across the width of the fabric. Sew the strips together end-to-end to make one long strip. Trim the borders from this strip. Refer to Borders (pg. 103) in the Construction Basics to measure and cut the outer borders. The strips are approximately 74½" for the sides and approximately 74½" for the top and bottom.

8 quilt and bind

Layer the quilt with batting and backing and quilt. After the quilting is complete, square up the quilt and trim away all excess batting and backing. Add binding to complete the quilt. See Construction Basics (pg. 103) for binding instructions.

61

For the tutorial and everything you need to make this quilt visit:
www.msqc.co/blockearlywinter17

62

windmill

When all the leaves have fallen and summer has faded to a distant memory, I poke my toes out from under my quilt in the morning and when I feel that chilly floor, I just want to snuggle right back under those covers and hibernate until spring! The truth is, I'm a California girl at heart and I love the feel of sunshine on my face. I adore being warm and I have a complicated relationship with Old Man Winter. But this year I'm trying something new. I'm going to try out a new trend called "hygge" and stop shivering!

The concept is simple enough. Hygge, pronounced "hoo-ga", is all about embracing the best of winter and creating a cozy, comfortable way of life. Picture this: the fireplace is glowing, the lights are low, candles are burning, a mug of hot cocoa is steaming next to you, and you are snuggled up beneath your favorite quilt with a good book. Now that's a trend I can get behind! I don't need to go to the store to create the perfect mood. All I need to do is put out a few more quilts—heaven knows I have plenty—stoke the fire, add a sweater to the mix, and really settle into the idea. I think in some ways we've all yearned to live this way more often when the season calls for it, but there's the issue of slowing down enough to do it!

Hygge isn't about having the hottest fur-covered pillows and designer antler furniture. It's a lifestyle that comes from the depths of Scandinavian winters. These happy people know the importance of making the most of what could be a miserable season. Instead, it becomes an opportunity to catch up on some reading, get closer to friends and family, and take things a bit slower. Getting caught up in the rush of everyday without pausing to relax is definitely something I'm going to try my best to avoid. It gives me the opportunity to dig out some hand stitching I've been meaning to get to and enjoy time with loved ones.

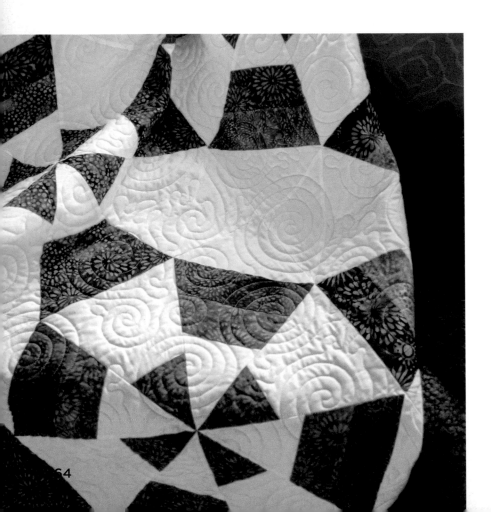

I think quilters are the kind of people who understand that good things take time. We practice this notion in our beautifully finished projects and now it's time to let that care for our craft seep into everyday life. Pause and let yourself enjoy this blustery, cold season. Watch the snow fall outside your window with a smile on your face and a scarf around your neck. As Edith Sitwell said, "Winter is the time for comfort, for good food and warmth, for the touch of a friendly hand and for a talk beside the fire: it is the time for home." There's so much to love at this time of year, dear quilters. I wish you the happiest of winters.

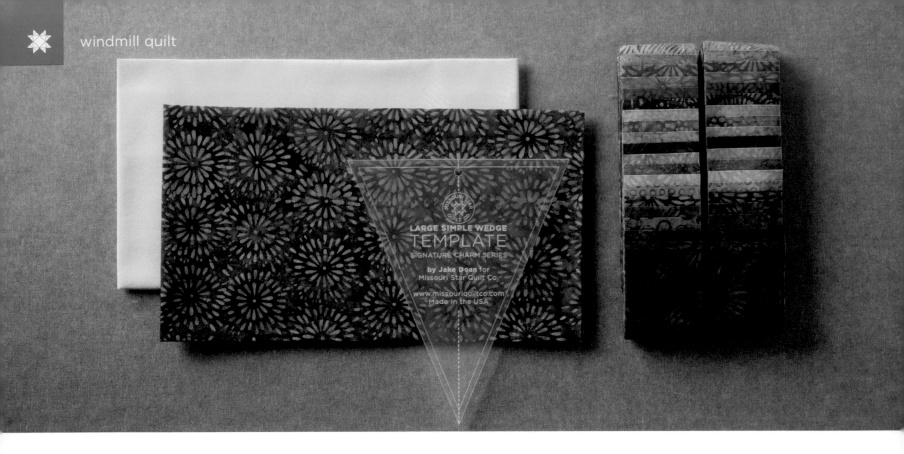

materials

QUILT SIZE
76" X 92"

BLOCK SIZE
16" finished

QUILT TOP
1 roll 2½" print strips
4½ yards background fabric

BORDER
1½ yards

BINDING
¾ yard

BACKING
5¾ yards - vertical seam(s)

OTHER
MSQC Large Simple Wedge Template

SAMPLE QUILT
Drizzle by Kathy Engle for Island Batiks

1 cut

From the background fabric, cut:

- (20) 5½" strips across the width of the fabric

- (7) 6" strips across the width of the fabric – subcut each strip into (6) 6" squares for a **total of 24**. Set 4 squares aside for another project. Cut each of the 20 squares from corner to corner once on the diagonal to **make 40** triangles.

2A

66

2B

2 make strip sets

Select 2 complimentary strips from the roll. Sew the strips together with right sides facing along the length. Add a 5½" background strip. Press the seam allowances toward the darker fabric. **Make 20** strip sets. 2A

Cut 8 triangles using the MSQC large simple wedge template across the width of each strip set. Flip the template 180 degrees with every other cut. You will have enough pieces to **make 20** blocks, keep all matching triangles stacked together. 2B

3 block construction

Block A

Choose a stack of 8 matching triangles. Sew 2 triangles together as shown. Repeat, as you sew the remaining triangles together in the stack. You will have 4 pairs. 3A

Sew 2 pairs together. Repeat for the remaining 2 pairs. You now have 2 halves of the block. 3B

Sew the 2 halves together. 3C

Sew a background 6" triangle to 4 corners of the block. Notice the background triangles are being sewn to triangles that have a colored strip on each corner. Press. 3D

Square up the block to 16½". **Make 10** A Blocks.

Block B

Make Block B in the same manner as Block A except the 6" background triangles are sewn to the portions of the block that have a background strip on the outer edge of the triangles. Press and square each block to 16½". **Make 10** B Blocks. 3E

Block size: 16" finished

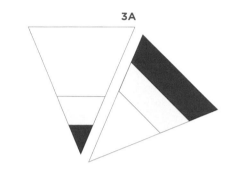

3A

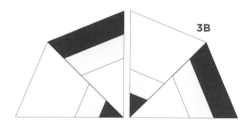

3B

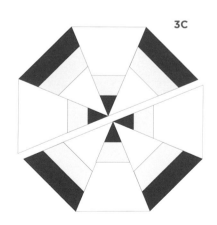

3C

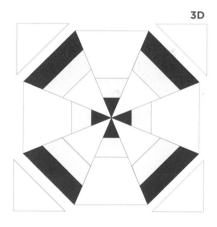

3D

3E

67

1 Select 2 complimentary 2½" strips. Sew them together with right sides facing along the length. Add a 5½" background strip. Cut 8 triangles using the MSQC large simple wedge template, flipping the template 180° with each cut. Keep all matching triangles together.

2 Choose 8 matching triangles. Sew 2 triangles together as shown. Repeat to make 4 pairs.

3 Sew 2 pairs together to make 1 half of the block. Repeat for the remaining 2 pairs to make the other half.

4 Sew the two halves together.

5 To make Block A, sew a 6" background triangle to each of the 4 striped portions of the block, thus creating a square. Square up the block to 16½". Make 10.

6 To make Block B, sew a 6" background triangle to each of the 4 background portions of the block, thus creating a square. Square up the block to 16½". Make 10.

4 arrange and sew

Lay out the blocks in rows. Each row is made up of 4 blocks with Block A and Block B alternating. Refer to the diagram on the left to see the layout, if necessary. **Make 5** rows. After the blocks have been sewn into rows, press the seam allowances of the odd-numbered rows toward the right and the even-numbered rows toward the left to make the seams "nest."

Sew the rows together to complete the center of the quilt.

5 border

Cut (8) 6½" strips across the width of the fabric. Sew the strips together end-to-end to make one long strip. Trim the borders from this strip.

Refer to Borders (pg. 103) in the Construction Basics to measure and cut the borders. The strips are approximately 80½" for the sides and approximately 76½" for the top and bottom.

6 quilt and bind

Layer the quilt with batting and backing and quilt. After the quilting is complete, square up the quilt and trim away all excess batting and backing. Add binding to complete the quilt. See Construction Basics (pg. 103) for binding instructions.

69

pineapple
table runner

When the snow falls and I'm in need of a midwinter pick-me-up, warm, cheesy fondue is at the top of my list. It feels so nostalgic and takes me right back to the early days of my marriage. Back then, fondue was the latest craze. Whenever people get married there are popular gifts that seem to be given in abundance. One year you might end up with three toasters, the next it might be a stack of waffle irons, and the year after that it could be an endless pile of towels. Well, when I was married it was fondue pots! We actually received six fondue pots of different makes and models in various earth tones. I kept the best one and returned the rest. From that moment on, fondue became a favorite in our family.

We loved fondue, but mostly we thought of it as a dessert. We would gather together around the fondue pot, melt chocolate inside, and dip all kinds of treats into that deep, rich pool of goodness—apple slices, pretzels,

70

For the tutorial and everything you need to make this quilt visit:
www.msqc.co/blockearlywinter17

71

marshmallows, strawberries, and even Rice Krispie Treats. But life tends to get busy, the beloved fondue pot got tucked away into a cupboard somewhere and, sadly, we stopped making fondue! Thankfully, the tradition has been revived and I couldn't be more enthusiastic about it the second time around. It seems that we've all been reawakened to the amazingness that is fondue.

For our anniversary last year, we wanted to do something different and Ron and I went out to eat at a fondue restaurant in Kansas City. I couldn't believe it, a restaurant just for fondue! The whole experience is so much fun. They seat you at a table that has a little burner built into the center and every course is fondue—and there were six courses! You know, all those years ago it never occurred to me that you could use the fondue pot for more than dessert. During that unforgettable dinner we had veggies and meats, bread and cheese, fruit and other sweets—all made in a fondue pot. What a memorable evening we had. Everything took longer as it was cooked at our table, but it caused us to relax and enjoy ourselves.

It's a simple thing to slow down and have a meal together as a family, but it makes all the difference. No matter how you do it, with or without a fondue pot, savor the time together and always have fun.

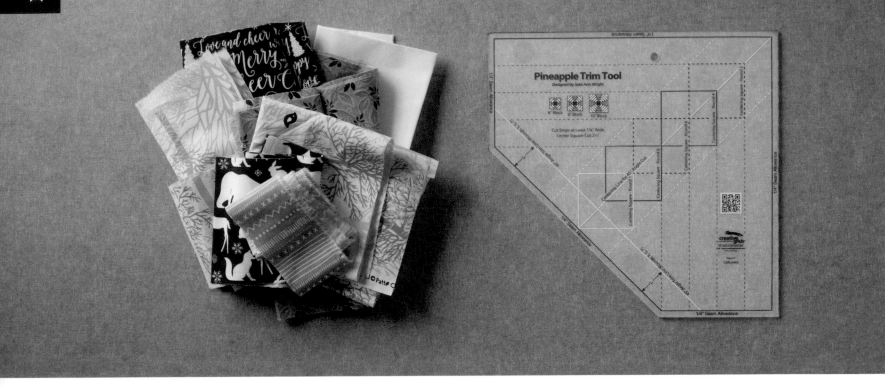

materials

TABLE RUNNER
18" x 40" finished

BLOCK SIZE
10" finished

TABLE RUNNER
¼ yard total of 2 assorted green prints*
½ yard total of 3 assorted red prints*
½ yard background fabric – includes sashing and inner border

OUTER BORDER
1½ yards – includes strips for outer round of blocks

BINDING
½ yard

BACKING
1½ yards

OTHER
Non-slip Pineapple Trim Tool by Creative Grids

Feel free to use any scraps you might have on hand. Just be sure to have enough fabric to cut all the pieces required.

1 cut

From the background fabric, cut:
- (9) 1½" x width of fabric strips – subcut the strips into the following pieces:
  - 1 strip into (6) 1½" x 3½" rectangles and (1) 10½" rectangle. Set the 1½" x 10½" rectangle aside for sashing.
  - 1 strip into (6) 1½" x 5½" rectangles.
  - 2 strips into (12) 1½" x 4½" rectangles and (1) 1½" x 10½" rectangle. Set the 1½" x 10½" rectangle aside for sashing.
  - 2 strips into (12) 1½" x 6" rectangles.

- 1 strip into (2) 1½" x 10½" rectangles. Set aside for sashing.

Reserve the remaining 2 strips for the inner border.

From green print #1, cut:
- (4) 2½" squares.

From green print #2, cut:
- (2) 1½" x width of fabric strips – subcut 1 strip into (6) 1½" x 5" rectangles and (1) 1½" x 7½" rectangle. Subcut the remaining strip into (5) 1½" x 7½" rectangles.

From the border fabric, cut:
- (2) 1½" x width of fabric

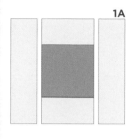

1A

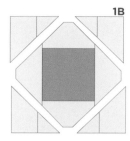

1B

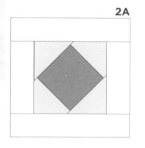

2A

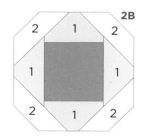

2B

```
2  1  2
1     1
2  1  2
```

3A

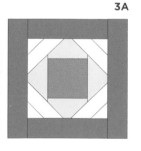

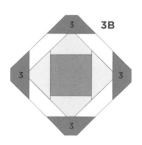

3B

```
   3
3     3
   3
```

4A

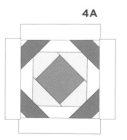

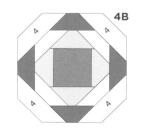

4B

strips – subcut the strips into
(6) 1½″ x 6½″ rectangles. Set
aside the remaining fabric for
the outer border.

From red print #1, cut:
- (2) 1½″ strips across the width
  of the fabric – subcut (1) strip
  into (6) 1½″ x 2½″ rectangles.
  Subcut the remaining strip into
  (6) 1½″ x 4¾″ rectangles.

From red print #2, cut:
- (2) 1½″ strips across the width
  of the fabric – subcut the strips
  into 1½″ x 4½″ rectangles. Each
  strip will yield 8 rectangles and
  a total of 12 are needed.

From red print #3, cut:
- (1) 5″ x width of fabric strip –
  subcut the strip into 5″ squares.
  The strip will yield 8 squares
  and a total of 6 are needed. Cut
  each of the 6 squares once
  on the diagonal to make (12) 5″
  triangles. **1A**

ROUND 1

When sewing the strips in place, use a
scant ¼″ seam allowance. Finger press
the seam allowances toward the added
strips. As each round of strips are added,
they may not overlap but, instead, create
a small space at the end of the strips. This
is nothing to be concerned about as the
space disappears as you trim. After each
round is added, press the unit with a hot
iron before trimming.

Sew: a red print 1½″ x 2½″ rectangle to
opposite sides of the center 2½″ square.

Add a 1½″ x 4¾″ matching red print
rectangle to the remaining 2 sides of the
square. **1A**

Trim: Place the white square marked
Centering Square – Round #1 on the
center square of the stitched unit. Trim all
4 sides. **1B**

ROUND 2

Sew: 1½″ x 3½″ background rectangles to
opposite sides of the trimmed unit. Sew
1½″ x 5½″ background rectangles onto
the remaining 2 sides. **2A**

Trim: Place the dashed square marked
Centering Square – Round #2 on the
center square of the unit.

Trim 2 sides, then turn the unit 180
degrees and trim the remaining 2 sides.
2B

ROUND 3

Sew: a matching green print
1½″ x 5″ rectangle to opposite sides
of the trimmed unit. Sew a 1½″ x 7½″
matching green print rectangle to the
remaining 2 sides. **3A**

Trim: Place the 45-degree white angle
line on the seam line of round #2. The
three angled white lines perpendicular
to the angled edge of the ruler are
additional guides to help position the
ruler for the remaining angled cuts. Trim
all four sides. **3B**

ROUND 4

Sew: 1½″ x 4½″ background rectangles
on each side of the trimmed unit. **4A**

Trim: Put the black solid square marked

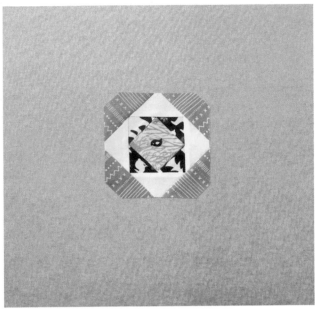

1 After sewing the appropriate rectangles to all 4 sides of the center square, trim using the white square marked "Centering Square – Round #1".

2 Add the background rectangles, trim following the directions on the ruler, then add the next round using a green print. Trim.

3 Add another round of background rectangles, trim following the directions on the ruler. Add the next round of red rectangles. Trim.

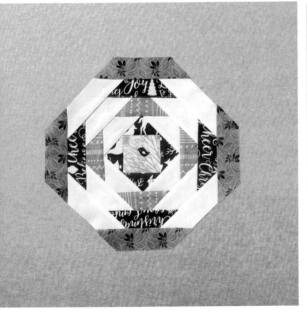

4 After adding another round of background rectangles and trimming, add the next round of prints. This time use the green rectangles that were cut from the border fabric. Trim.

5 Stitch a 5" red triangle to each corner of the block.

6 Complete the block by placing the black solid square marked Centering Square – Round #8 and trimming on all four sides of the block.

76

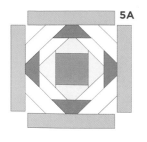
5A

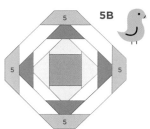
5B

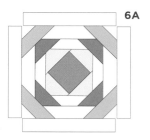
6A

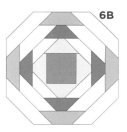
6B

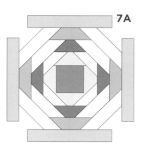
7A

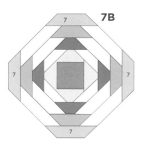
7B

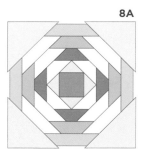
8A

8B

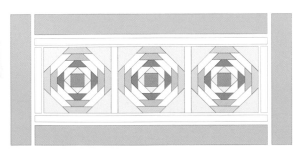

NOTE: *The angled white lines are used when trimming rounds 3, 5 and 7.*

Centering Square – Round #4 on the center square of the trimmed unit. Trim 2 sides, then turn the unit 180-degrees and trim the two remaining sides. **4B**

ROUND 5

Sew: matching red print 1½" x 4½" rectangles to each side of the trimmed unit. **5A**

Trim: Place the 45-degree white angle line on the seam line of round #4 and trim all 4 sides. **5B**

ROUND 6

Sew: 1½" x 6" background rectangles to each side of the trimmed unit. **6A**

Trim: Place the black dashed square marked Centering Square – Round #6 on the center square of the stitched unit. Trim 2 sides, then turn the unit 180-degrees and trim the remaining 2 sides. **6B**

ROUND 7

Sew: a 1½" x 6½" matching green print rectangle to each side of the trimmed unit. **7A**

Trim: Place the white 45-degree angle line on the **seam line of round #6**. Trim all four sides. **7B**

8 COMPLETE THE BLOCK

Sew: a matching 5" print triangle onto each corner of the trimmed unit. **8A**

Trim: Place the black solid square marked **Centering Square – Round #8** on the center square of the sewn unit. Trim 2

sides, then turn the unit 180-degrees and trim the remaining 2 sides.
Make 3 blocks. **8B**

Block size: 10" finished

2 arrange and sew

Lay out the blocks in 1 row. Add a 1½" x 10½" background sashing strip between each block and at each end of the row as you sew the blocks together.

3 inner border

Pick up the (2) 1½" x width of fabric strips that were set aside for the inner border. Measure the table runner through the center and trim 2 strips to that length. They should measure approximately 34½". Sew one to each side (long edges) of the runner.

4 outer border

Cut (3) 3½" strips across the width of the fabric. Sew the strips together end-to-end to make one long strip. Trim the borders from this strip.

Refer to Borders (pg. 103) in the Construction Basics to measure and cut the outer borders. The strips are approximately 34½" for the sides and approximately 18½" for the top and bottom (short ends).

5 quilt and bind

Layer the table runner with batting and backing and quilt. After the quilting is complete, square up the runner and trim away all excess batting and backing. Add binding to complete the quilt. See Construction Basics (pg. 103) for binding instructions.

For the tutorial and everything you need to make this quilt visit:

www.msqc.co/blockearlywinter17

dresden zippered pouch

Christmas is the most magical time of year, but that magic doesn't happen by chance; it's a lot of work! You see, if I want to enjoy a beautifully decorated house, I've got to haul the Christmas boxes up from the storage room and spend an entire weekend setting out my Christmas village. If I want to surprise my neighbors with gingerbread cookies, it's up to me to mix and bake and ice those sweet little cookie men. And if I want my family to experience Christmas morning magic, well, I've got to shop, sew, and wrap until I've prepared something special for each and every person on my list. Add that to the fact that my December calendar is always bursting at the seams with concerts and parties, and I often find myself too busy to actually enjoy the festivities.

Years ago, a sweet friend taught me a great lesson about savoring the magic of Christmas time. Evelyn was a young mother who struggled to balance the daily to-do list with the desire to savor every precious moment with her children. As Christmas drew near, Evelyn had visions of cutting out paper snowflakes and making ice cream out of newly fallen snow. The reality was, however, that she was much too busy with laundry, diapers, and holiday errands of all sorts to even get started on her list of Christmas fun.

Then, as luck would have it, Evelyn stumbled and broke a small bone in her foot. With a preschooler, a toddler, and a babe in arms to care for, life came to a screeching halt. Her daily to-do list was tossed aside, and a new normal took over. Every morning her mother would arrive before breakfast. She helped Evelyn into the car, buckled up the kids, and grabbed all the dirty laundry from the day before.

For two weeks, Evelyn lounged in her parents' living room with her foot elevated as her mother fed and bathed and played with those three babies. Dirty clothes were washed daily. Healthy dinners were provided. At first Evelyn was delighted to let go of her responsibilities, but it wasn't long before she started to feel a bit antsy. As crazy as it seemed, she actually missed her to-do list. During that

two-week sabbatical, Evelyn came to realize that there is magic in the everyday happenings of life. It isn't always necessary to create big, fancy experiences in order for the holidays to be special. Because, like it or not, life doesn't slow down just because it's Christmas.

When Evelyn's foot was healed well enough for her to manage on her own, she picked right up where she had left off with dishes, diapers, and slobbery kisses. Some days the kitchen was clean. Other days they abandoned the mess to make snow angels. "It's all about balance and expectations," Evelyn told me. She realized that happiness is found in simple things.

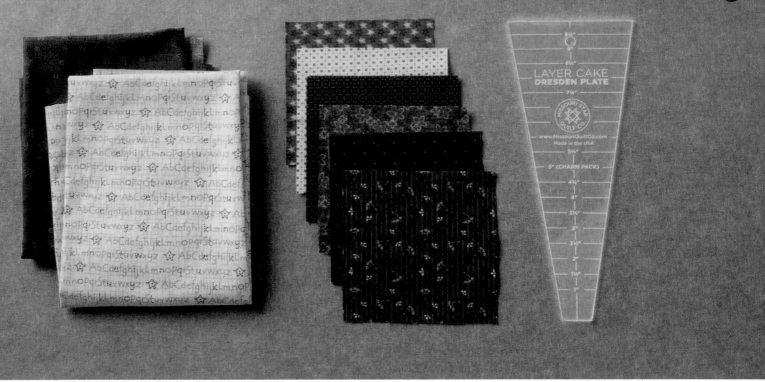

materials

DRESDEN ZIPPERED POUCH
Finished Size: approximately 8½" x 9"

SUPPLY LIST
(4 - 8) 5" print squares
(1) 5½" x 20" rectangle
(2) 2½" x 20" contrasting strips
(1) 9" x 20" rectangle - lining
(1) 9" x 20" rectangle fusible batting
nylon zipper
MSQC Dresden Plate Template

ZIPPERED GIFT CARD POUCH
Finished Size: 3½" x 4½"

SUPPLY LIST
4½" x 10½" rectangle
4½" x 10½" rectangle - lining
4½" x 10½" rectangle fusible batting
nylon zipper

SAMPLE QUILT
Berries and Blossoms from Zentex

 NOTE: *You can make the bags any size you choose. The sizes of fabric given are just guidelines.*

1 cut

From the 5" squares, cut 8 wedges using the MSQC Dresden Plate template. Align the 5" mark on the template with the edge of a square. Cut 1 then flip the template 180 degrees and cut another.

 NOTE: *If you want your Dresden to be real scrappy, use a different square for each wedge.* **1A**

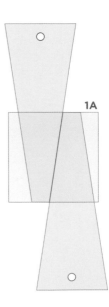

82

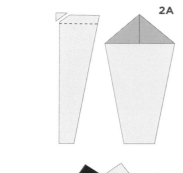

2A

2B

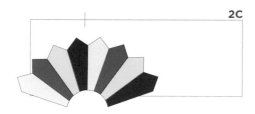

2C

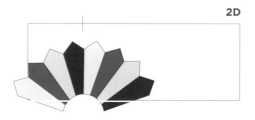

2D

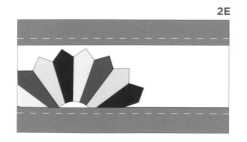

2E

2 sew

Fold a wedge in half lengthwise with right sides together. Sew across the top (the widest part), then clip the seam allowance at a 45-degree angle. Turn the point right side out. Press, centering the seam. **Make 8.** 2A

Sew the wedges together to make an arc. 2B

Measure 5" in from one edge of the 5½" x 20" rectangle. Mark that point with a pin then place the center of the arc at the 5" point and pin in place. The top of the small arc at the bottom of the Dresden will be aligned with the edge of the rectangle. **Note:** you will be trimming some of the bottom edges of the Dresden arc off. 2C

Appliqué the arc in place using a buttonhole stitch.

Trim the arc evenly with the bottom of the rectangle. 2D

Press the fusible fleece or batting to the reverse side of the lining fabric. Center the 5½" x 20" rectangle on top of the fleece, right side up. Align a 2½" contrasting strip along the top edge of the rectangle with right sides facing. Sew in place through all the layers. Repeat for the remaining 2½" strip, stitching it to the bottom of the rectangle. Press the strips toward the outer edges of the fleece. Topstitch ¼" away from the seam lines. 2E

Notice the piece is all quilted and ready to be sewn into a bag.

Trim off any selvages and straighten any uneven edges.

Cut the rectangle in half vertically to make (2) 9" x 9½" - 10" rectangles. Set aside while you prepare the zipper.

3 prepare the zipper

Cut (1) 1½" x 5" strip of fabric. Fold it in half and press. Open and fold in the two long sides toward the center and press again. This is the tab that will go on both ends of the zipper. 3A

Trim off the bottom of the zipper. Slide the zipper end into the fold of the tab. Top stitch through all three layers. Trim the tab to fit the end of the zipper. 3B

Lay the zipper along the side of the bag. Slide back the zipper head so the zipper is open. Then trim it so it is 1" shorter than the opening of the bag. Slip the open ends of the zipper into the fold of the tab. Sew across the end of the tab in the same manner as before and, trim the ends of the tab to fit the width of the zipper. 3C

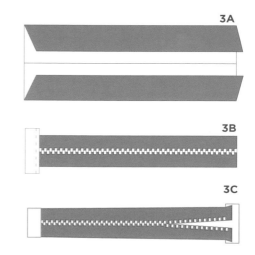

3A

3B

3C

83

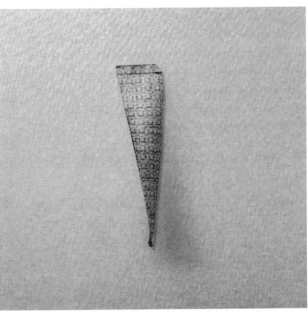

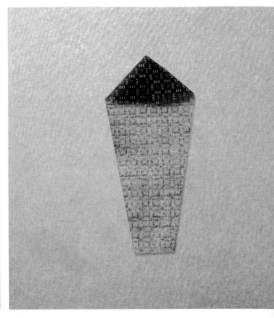

1 Align the 5" mark of the MSQC Dresden Plate template with the edge of a 5" square. Cut a wedge using a rotary cutter.

2 Fold each wedge in half with right sides facing. Sew across the widest part of the piece. Clip the seam allowance at a 45° angle.

3 Turn the point right side out. Press, centering the seam.

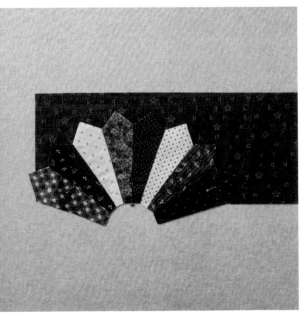

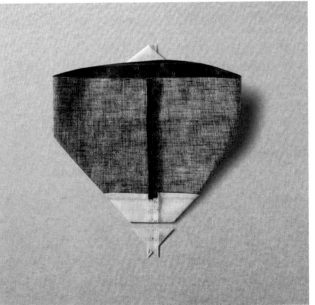

4 Sew 8 wedges together to make an arc. Pin the Dresden in place and stitch to the background fabric using a buttonhole stitch or small zig zag.

5 Open the bag, align the side seam of the bag with the bottom seam. Sew straight across about 1" from the point. Trim the excess fabric ¼" away from the sewn seam. Boxing the corners will make the bag stand upright.

6 Turn the bag right side out.

84

4A

4 sew

Place the zipper face down on the edge of the right side of one of the pieces of the pouch. Remember, the zipper is about 1" shorter than the opening so it will need to be centered in that space (½" in on either end). Stitch in place. As you approach the head of the zipper, raise the presser foot of the sewing machine and slide the zipper head down past the foot. Lower the presser foot and continue sewing to the end. Fold the sewn edge of the zipper toward the inside of the bag and topstitch along the edge. 4A

Repeat the above instructions to install the zipper on the other side of the bag.

4B

Open the zipper. Put the right sides of the bag together. Is the zipper open? If it's not, you will have no way to turn the bag right side out. Come in just inside the ½" mark and sew down one side, across the bottom and up the remaining side. After you have sewn the seams, go back and use a zig zag stitch to finish the raw edges of the seams. 4B

If you would like to have the bag to have a flat bottom, align the side seam of the bag with the bottom seam. Sew straight across about 1" from the point. Repeat for the other side of the bag. Trim the pointed edge off and turn the bag right side out. 4C

zippered gift card pouch

1 press and quilt

Press the fusible fleece or batting to the reverse side of the lining fabric. Center the 4½" rectangle you're using for the outside of the bag on top of the fleece, right side up. Quilt the three layers together by making straight rows of stitching ⅜" to ½" apart.

Trim the quilted piece to 4" x 10" after quilting.

Cut the quilted rectangle in half vertically to make (2) 4" x 5" pieces. Follow the instructions for preparing and installing the zipper and stitching the bag together.

Insert gift card of your choice.

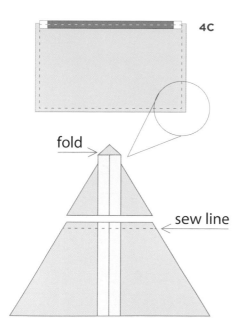

4C

fold

sew line

85

stitch away stress

One of my favorite things to do on a chilly, winter night is snuggle up next to my husband on the couch and knit a scarf while we watch a movie together. It's simple, but it makes all the cares of the day disappear. Give knitting a try if you haven't yet and you might find a fun, creative outlet to keep your hands busy and your mind at ease.

Have you ever heard the phrase "Sewing mends the soul"? Knitting is just as therapeutic and can help soothe away stress with every stitch. At the start of this new year, make a resolution you'll love to keep and won't leave you worried if you skip a day. As a quilter, chances are you've already crossed over into the world of fiber arts and knitting is a wonderful place to begin your journey if you're considering a new kind of project.

Most people start with a simple scarf and soon find themselves neck deep in afghans, baby blankets, hats, mittens, slippers, shawls, and sweaters. The great thing about knitting, just like sewing, is that once you've learned a skill well enough for it to be repetitive, it allows your mind to relax. And another awesome benefit is, when you're all through, you get something beautiful and useful out of the process.

The satisfaction of making a practical and attractive item with your own two hands is like nothing else. Being creative is an important part of mental health and knitting is a wonderful outlet for so many reasons. Begin this year with a stress-reducing project and knit yourself a lovely scarf. When you wear it around, you'll feel proud of your accomplishment and warm and snuggly all winter long.

long winter wrap scarf

pattern design by Janet Yamamoto
pattern writer by Jenny Fish

size: Adult 9' long, including fringe, by 8" wide.

materials

1 Wool-Ease Thick & Quick - Grass Yarn (Super bulky weight) 6oz./170g (106 yd/97m) ball

1 Wool-Ease Thick & Quick - Wheat Yarn (Super bulky weight) 6oz./170g (106 yd/97m) ball

Size 13US Circular Knitting Needles with a 29" cable or longer

Long Tail Cast-On

Start by making a slip knot about 4 yards in for the scarf. Place the slip knot on needle and hold it in your right hand. Make sure that the yarn tail is pointing toward you. Insert your left thumb and index finger between your two strands of yarn. Close the rest of your fingers around the yarn. Insert the needle under the strand that is wrapped around your thumb. Scoop up the strand that is wrapped around your index finger. Bring your yarn out through the thumb loop. Pull your thumb from the loop of the yarn and pull the yarn to tighten the new stitch. Repeat until you have 200 stitches for this scarf.

Scarf

Using the Long Tail Cast-On cast on 200 stitches in MC (main color). If you start about 3 yards in you should have enough of the tail to complete the 200 stitches. This will give you a 9 foot scarf. If you would like the scarf to be shorter cast on fewer stitches.

Row 1: Knit across, cut yarn leaving an 8" tail. Attach CC (contrasting color) leaving an 8" tail and tie a knot right at the end of the row. This will become your fringe.

Row 2: Knit across and attach MC as in row 1.

Repeat Row 1 and Row 2 changing yarn color after each row. End with CC.

Bind off

Bind off in desired method with CC.

The Forest Bride
By Nichole Spravzoff

THE WEDDING

Ingrid kept a close watch on Gustav throughout the night. He finally slept after his foot was set and he was given a heavy dose of bitters. She slept in her rocking chair next to the fire with Otto at her feet, waking occasionally as the burning logs popped and the house creaked. Late in the night Gustav cried out for her.

Quickly wrapping her dressing gown around herself, she poked her head in the doorway and watched him for any sign of discomfort. He shifted and spoke her name, "Ingrid?"

"Yes?" She responded.

He seemed to be fast asleep, but then he whispered in a thick, gravelly voice, "I need you."

"What do you need? Water? More blankets?" She tried to guess at his meaning, but he drifted off again. She went to the stove and set the tea kettle on to boil. When it was ready, she returned to his room with a mug of honey-sweetened blackcurrant tea and some dry biscuits on a tray. Setting it on the bedside table, she unfolded

a quilt at the foot of the bed and draped it carefully over him. When she was through, his hand flopped out beneath the covers. Ingrid tried again. "Would you like some tea?" She asked softly.

Gustav reached out and caught ahold of her dressing gown. All he said was, "You."

"Here's some tea," she said. He didn't respond, but his hand found hers. He squeezed her hand with surprising strength and then his fingers slipped away again and he was fast asleep.

Ingrid left the tea next to his bedside and returned to her rocking chair, replaying what had just happened in her mind. The fire was reduced to coals, but she felt a warmth spread throughout her body, as if it still blazed brightly.

In a matter of a few days, Gustav was able to move about again and he returned home to finish recuperating. Although it hadn't been a very restful week sleeping in her rocking chair, Ingrid missed having him around. At first it was unnerving, having him in her home, but soon his presence felt welcome, even necessary. Each day they had talked while she sewed. They spoke at length about their families, their childhoods, the games they played as children, their fears, and even the things they hoped for. There had never been a person who spoke to her as candidly as he did, except for her mother. At first he had been cautious and stoic, as he had been in public, but his outward demeanor melted away as he lay in bed with his foot propped up, drinking tea. And so did hers.

When he left, her cabin felt large for the first time in her life. The walls practically echoed with his absence. He'd promised to return as soon as his foot healed, but that might take weeks. Meanwhile, Karl's wedding was soon approaching and Gustav would be caught up in the preparations with his family. Karl was marrying Lottie, a frivolous young girl who had been making eyes at him for years. She was at least ten years his junior, but believed herself to be very mature. Ingrid was asked to add some embellishment to her wedding frock and had ascertained all of this while listening to her. It was all Ingrid could do to stifle a laugh as Lottie prattled on about the arrangements—how she would wear her hair, what flowers would be used in the decorations, and how extensive the smorgasbord would be. Ingrid quickly pinned up the hem of Lottie's dress, avoiding her delicate ankles, and added a ruffle here and a tuck there as directed.

The sky was darkening when Lottie finally exited Ingrid's cabin in a flurry of last-minute requests for the gown, leaving her to the final preparations. Ingrid sighed deeply as she sat in her

88

rocking chair with Lottie's wedding dress on her lap. She'd never owned such an extravagant dress. It was a beautiful, showy gown, exquisitely made by a professional dressmaker in Skogsmark. It didn't need a thing more added to it, despite Lottie's many suggestions for improvement. Changing it was practically a crime, but Ingrid did as she was told and added a few more frills. It was careful, slow work, but she would have it done in time for the wedding.

* * *

The night before Karl's wedding, thick, white flakes fell in abundance, blown about by the wind. Winter seemed to have returned with a vengeance, eager to bury the delicate green shoots that had dared to break through the rich, black soil. Karl was surrounded by a boisterous crowd of fellow woodcutters who were chanting incessantly for him to take yet another drink. He humored them and grinned widely as he gulped from the deep flagon, trying to hold back the tide of unwelcome thoughts that were bombarding his mind.

"Congratulations, Big Brother!" Gustav broke through the roar of the crowd and hooked his arm around Karl's neck, pulling him closer. "I'm so happy for you," he shouted, a little too close to Karl's ear.

"Thanks," he said, frowning momentarily as he looked down into Gustav's overjoyed face. "Another round for everyone!" He shouted to the whole group, who responded with a resounding cheer. He pulled away from Gustav and grabbed another tankard of ale, downing it recklessly. It streamed out the sides of his mouth and down his chin. He sat down heavily and the world went black.

When he awoke, the night was so dark, he couldn't see his hand in front of his face. It took him a while to realize he had a blindfold on. "Hey! Where am I?" He shouted.

His friends responded with a smattering of suppressed laughter. "He has no idea where he is!" One whispered through a horse-like chuckle.

"Shh! Don't say anything!" Another said, giggling and snorting at the same time.

It was a tradition in the village that on the night before a wedding, the engaged couple would be kidnapped by their friends and led on a wild-goose chase to ensure they were a proper match for each other. The kidnapping was always good-natured and never involved any actual geese, but tonight's kidnapping made Karl agitated.

"Okay, guys, enough is enough." He growled.

"Oooh! Someone's got his knickers in a knot!" A voice called out.

Karl wheeled around, looking for someone to strike, but missed. Then he tripped on the icy snow beneath him and landed squarely on his rear. Now his trousers were soaked through and his temper took a turn for the worse. "That's it!" He clenched his fists and began swinging blindly. A firm hand grabbed his arm and tried to lift him to his feet. He swiftly found his mark and heard a stifled gasp. "Gustav? Is that you?"

"Yes," Gustav wheezed.

Karl stopped swinging and let his arms drop to his sides. He paused before pulling off his blindfold and winced at the scene before him.

"Go home, guys. I think it's time to call it a night," Gustav croaked out. He cautiously edged closer to Karl.

Karl blinked slowly, watching his friends turn and walk away. They were standing right in front of Lottie's house. A candle burned in the window, but he didn't see any movement inside. He glanced over at Gustav, who was propped up on a wooden crutch with his hand over his stomach. Gustav didn't look angry, but he was wary of what Karl would do next.

"I'm sorry about all this," Gustav gestured to Karl's friends who were now out of earshot.

"Why are you apologizing to me?" Karl said.

"I told them not to kidnap you. It's just a silly tradition," he said. Karl shook his head. "This isn't right."

"I know, I told them ..." Gustav tried to continue apologizing.

"Don't. You don't need to say you're sorry," Karl insisted. "This whole thing is wrong."

"What, about the wedding?" Gustav asked.

"There won't be a wedding," Karl declared firmly.

Abruptly, the sound of an injured animal rang out through the chilly air. It made Karl and Gustav pause as it intensified, becoming more fierce until it sounded like a human shriek.

"What could that be?" Gustav wondered.

"It sounds like it might be a lynx. Stay close," Karl cautioned. Lottie lept out from behind a tree and pummeled Karl with all of her might. She kicked and scratched and even pulled his hair. Gustav kept his distance, trying to find a way to intervene before Karl got too banged up.

"What are you doing!" Karl finally managed to subdue Lottie. He had her arms pinned to her sides, but her feet kept moving as she tried to kick him repeatedly. "Stop it!" He roared. But she was too fast, her narrow boot shot out from under her skirts and she kicked him right where she had intended. Karl let go of her instantly and slumped over in the snow.

Lottie looked over Karl with a satisfied expression and kicked snow in his face. "When were you going to tell me?" She seethed. "I heard everything you said."

"I'm sorry. So sorry," Karl stammered.

"Well, that's fine. There's plenty of rich, handsome men in Skogsmark." She sniffed and checked her nails for any damage before she turned away, enjoying the view of Karl on the ground for a moment longer.

"Lottie, this wasn't about you," Karl tried to explain.

"That's even worse," she shot back. The silhouette of Lottie's father appeared in the doorway. He was clearly holding a rifle.

"Do you need help, Sweetheart?" He threatened.

"No, Papa," she said sweetly. Then she turned back to Karl. "I'd leave quickly if I were you." She slammed the door for effect and then she was gone. The candle was snuffed out and Karl and Gustav were alone again in the dark. They looked at one another in shock, but then Karl grinned.

"I deserved that," he admitted.

"If anyone asks, I'll tell them you survived a fight with a wolverine," Gustav quipped. Then they both laughed in earnest at the entire disastrous night. It had been a complete mess, but rightfully so. Karl had a lot of amends to make, and he was beginning right then and there with his brother. As they trudged home through the slush and the mud, Karl told him everything and Gustav listened intently. Karl knew he couldn't make up for his misdeeds with one confession, but he was determined to make everything right.

* * *

The day of the wedding, Ingrid prepared to bring the dress over to Lottie, who would be too busy to come pick it up herself. Before she could bundle up to leave the house, she heard a knock at the door. Otto howled in anticipation of company. Maybe they had sent someone over to fetch the dress. She opened the door to find Karl, who looked a little worse for wear. His eye was blackened and he had scratches all over his face. That won't do for a groom, she thought to herself, but smiled thinly as she greeted him. "Good morning, Karl. I'm guessing you're here to pick up Lottie's dress?"

She went to retrieve it and he stopped her.

"No, that's not why I'm here," he said, with a mischievous grin on his face.

Ingrid was puzzled. "Should I bring the dress to her?" She guessed.

"No, no. She won't be needing it today," he began.

Otto sniffed Karl's hand, looking for something to eat and licked his fingers. "Down, Otto," she said. Turning her attention back to Karl, Ingrid blurted out, "So, why are you here?" and then flushed at her own impudence.

"I'm here because there's about to be a wedding with no bride," Karl smiled and leaned toward her.

Ingrid was aghast, "Why are you looking at me that way? I won't marry you!"

Karl laughed loudly at her outburst and bent over to catch his breath. "I don't want to marry you," he said, "but I'm pretty sure my brother does."

Her words caught in her throat and she couldn't speak. Otto took this moment to jump up on Karl and continue his search for food. He began howling again when he located a packet of jerky in Karl's breast pocket.

Karl obliged and fed Otto strips of jerky until Ingrid found the ability to speak again. "How do you know he wants to marry me?" She ventured.

"Sorry. I was in such a hurry, I forgot to give you this," Karl reached into the same pocket the jerky had been in and pulled out a crumpled note that looked like it had once been carefully folded. He handed it to her casually, but his grin widened when she opened it and began reading. Her fingers started to tremble. Tears streaked down her face and she wiped them away with her sleeve.

"Is it a good note?" He asked with the most genuine smile she'd ever seen on his face. This wasn't a joke. It wasn't Karl coming to torment her. He was being sincere. It astonished her almost as much as Gustav's note had.

"Yes, it's a good note," she sniffed and smiled back.

"What should I tell him?" He cocked his head and looked at her knowingly.

"Let me write a reply," she requested.

"Go right ahead." He nodded to her and waited while she took a few minutes to write multiple drafts of her response.

When she finally handed the note to him, Otto had his fill of jerky and lay at Karl's feet, wagging his tail. Karl motioned as if he

90

would put the note into his pocket, but opened it up instead and scanned it quickly. "Just as I thought." He smirked, looking quite pleased. "I'll give him your answer shortly."

"Hey!" Ingrid exclaimed. "That's private." She reached for the note, but Karl placed his hand over his pocket and patted it.

"Don't worry. It's safe with me." He winked at her. "I'll come pick you up this afternoon."

She nodded, smiling as she shut the door behind him, trying to calm herself, but it was no use. When he was out of sight, she collapsed into a heap with her back against the door and cried out of sheer joy with her face tucked into her knees. Otto nudged her with his nose and she rubbed his ears. "It's time, Otto. Now, where's Mother's dress?"

It was tucked away in the furthest reaches of the cedar chest, wrapped carefully in thin paper and tied up with a silken cord. Her mother's wedding gown was now almost thirty years old, but it was well-preserved. The cream-colored lace had not yellowed and the ribbon around the waist only needed a light pressing. It was not the current fashion, but it was lovely with a wide neckline to accent her collarbones and tiers of delicate tulle that made it appear weightless. As she was in the middle of pressing the dress, her sweet neighbor, Marta, knocked hurriedly on the door. She lumbered in, red in the face and perspiring, her swollen belly making it difficult to walk. She talked animatedly as she shooed Otto out of the way and began fussing with Ingrid's dress. "What do you think you're doing? You can't get ready without me!" She said as she gathered Ingrid into a deep embrace.

"How did you know?" Ingrid said as they laughed together with arms resting on each other's shoulders.

"I knew this day was coming sooner than later," she mused. "Watching the way that boy acted around you, it was clear. He would have broken his other ankle if it meant you'd say yes."

She chattered on, somehow aware of the entire situation surrounding Karl canceling the wedding, Lottie's hostile reaction, and Gustav's last-minute proposal via letter. Ingrid marveled at Marta's ability to scrape together all the village gossip and arrive at the very moment when she was needed. By early afternoon, she had Ingrid laced securely into her gown, pressed and powdered to perfection, with a mass of dark curls atop her head, ringed with a crown of spring flowers from the forest. Ingrid glanced over at Lottie's untouched wedding dress hanging heavily from the rafters and felt a sharp pang of sympathy for the girl. Someday Lottie

would marry the right person for her, but today was not that day.

The sun glinted brightly on the rapidly melting snow when Ingrid set off to the chapel with Karl at the reins of the carriage and Marta in the back, still fussing over Ingrid's dress and fanning herself after a busy morning. Gustav was not allowed to ride along because it was bad luck to see a bride before the wedding. She had tucked his note into one of her fur-lined mittens and smiled to herself, knowing it was there.

The carriage arrived at the church and was at once surrounded by murmuring villagers. Ingrid paused, feeling anxious with all their wondering eyes fixed on her. Her smile momentarily faded until she saw Gustav burst through the wide church doors and rush toward her as fast as he could possibly go on his injured foot.

"You're here," he breathed out, reaching for her.

"I am," she smiled again and removed her mitten before taking his hand. He felt the note clutched in her palm and grinned up at her. "Isn't it bad luck for you to see me?" She hinted.

"I don't believe in superstition," he remarked, and led her down the aisle.

The villagers filed in after them and, placated by the comfort of tradition, watched admiringly as they were wed. After all, there would still be a wedding party to attend later on. Finally, the priest declared them married and they shared their first kiss. Ingrid blushed deeply and buried her head in Gustav's shoulder.

"Do you want to know a secret?" He said.

Ingrid said nothing, but grinned to herself and nodded against his chest.

"At the feast, the direction the tree fell wasn't an accident," he said quickly.

She jerked away from him and let out a gasp. "What are you talking about?" She thumped him lightly on the chest and he grimaced. "You mean you did it on purpose?" Her voice was a mix of surprise and shock.

"I notched the trunk to make sure it would fall toward the woods," he admitted.

Her eyes widened. "Let's keep that between us," she whispered. He nodded in agreement and they left the chapel together, hand in hand.

block of the month

Quilt Size: 87" x 87"

SUPPLY LIST

INNER BORDER
½ yard

OUTER BORDER
1½ yards

BINDING
¾ yard

BACKING
2¾ yards 108" wide

inner border

Cut (8) 2½" strips across the width of the fabric. Sew the strips together end-to-end to make one long strip. Trim the borders from this strip.

Refer to Borders (pg. 103) in the Construction Basics to measure and cut the inner borders. The strips are approximately 72½" for the sides and approximately 76½" for the top and bottom.

outer border

Cut 9 – 6" strips across the width of the fabric. Sew the strips together end-to-end to make one long strip. Trim the borders from this strip.

Refer to Borders (pg. 103) in the Construction Basics to measure and cut the outer borders. The strips are approximately 76½" for the sides and approximately 87½" for the top and bottom.

quilt and bind

Layer the quilt with batting and backing and quilt. After the quilting is complete, square up the quilt and trim away all excess batting and backing. Add binding to complete the quilt. See Construction Basics (pg. 103) for binding instructions.

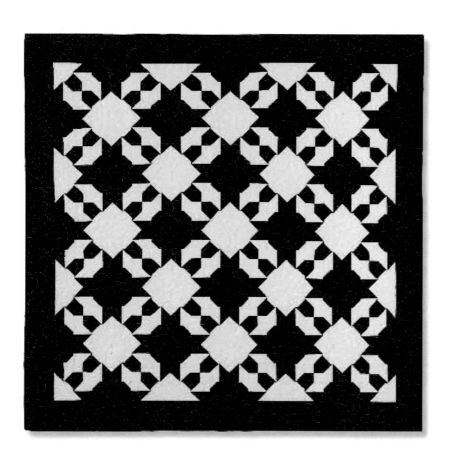

disappearing hourglass 3

QUILT SIZE
78″ x 78″ finished

BLOCK SIZE
11¼″ finished

QUILT TOP
1 package of 10″ background
    squares
1 package of 10″ solid squares

OUTER BORDER
1½ yards

BINDING
¾ yard

BACKING
5 yards – vertical seam(s)

SAMPLE QUILT
Bella Solids Black by Moda Fabrics
Bella Solids White by Moda Fabrics

QUILTING PATTERN
Arc Doodle

ONLINE TUTORIALS
msqc.co/blockearlywinter17

PATTERN
pg. 6

dreamweaver

QUILT SIZE
73" x 82"

BLOCK SIZE
8" finished

QUILT TOP
1 roll of 2½" print strips
1¼ yards background fabric
1½ yards sashing - includes inner
    border
¼ yard for cornerstones

OUTER BORDER
1¼ yards

BINDING
¾ yard

BACKING
5 yards - vertical seam(s)

SAMPLE QUILT
Atelier de France by French General
for Moda Fabrics

QUILTING PATTERN
Paisley Feathers

ONLINE TUTORIALS
msqc.co/blockearlywinter17

PATTERN
pg. 14

pineapple table runner

TABLE RUNNER
18" x 40" finished

BLOCK SIZE
10" finished

TABLE RUNNER
¼ yard total of 2 assorted green
  prints*
½ yard total of 3 assorted red prints*
½ yard background fabric – includes
  sashing and inner border

OUTER BORDER
1½ yards – includes strips for outer
round of blocks

BINDING
½ yard

BACKING
1½ yards

OTHER
Non-slip Pineapple Trim Tool by
Creative Grids

*Feel free to use any scraps you might have on
hand. Just be sure to have enough fabric to cut
all the pieces required.

QUILTING PATTERN
Sticky Buns

ONLINE TUTORIALS
msqc.co/blockearlywinter17

PATTERN
pg. 70

roundabout

QUILT SIZE
61" X 70"

BLOCK SIZE
9" finished

QUILT TOP
2 packages 5" print squares
1¾ yards background fabric
– includes inner border

OUTER BORDER
1¼ yards

BINDING
¾ yard

BACKING
4 yards - horizontal seam(s)

SAMPLE QUILT
Sorbet by Leonie Bateman for
Penny Rose Fabrics

QUILTING PATTERN
Free Swirls

ONLINE TUTORIALS
msqc.co/blockearlywinter17

PATTERN
pg. 22

stars & pinwheels

QUILT SIZE
80" x 92"

BLOCK SIZE
12" finished

SUPPLIES
1 package 10" print squares*
5½ yards background fabric
– includes pieced inner border

*Make sure the print squares you choose
contrast with the background fabric.*

OUTER BORDER
2 yards

BINDING
¾ yard

BACKING
7½ yards - horizontal seam(s)

SAMPLE QUILT
Bloomsbury by Franny & Jane
for Moda Fabrics

QUILTING PATTERN
Cotton Candy

ONLINE TUTORIALS
msqc.co/blockearlywinter17

PATTERN
pg. 38

97

sweet blend

QUILT SIZE
64" X 73"

BLOCK SIZE
9" finished

SUPPLY LIST
3¼ yards dark solid
1 package of 10" background squares
  plus 2½ yards **or** 5¼ yards background fabric - includes borders

BINDING
¾ yard

BACKING
4½ yards - vertical seam(s)

OTHER
Easy Circle Cut Ruler
3¼ yards 24" wide fusible interfacing

SAMPLE QUILT
Kona Cotton Regal Solids
by Robert Kaufman Fabrics
Kona Cotton White Solids
by Robert Kaufman Fabrics

QUILTING PATTERN
Loops & Swirls

ONLINE TUTORIALS
msqc.co/blockearlywinter17

PATTERN
pg. 30

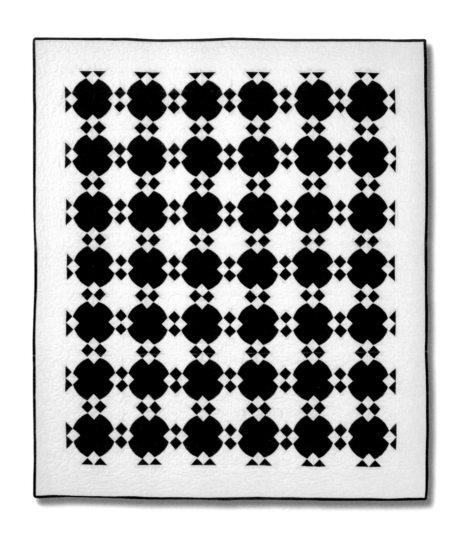

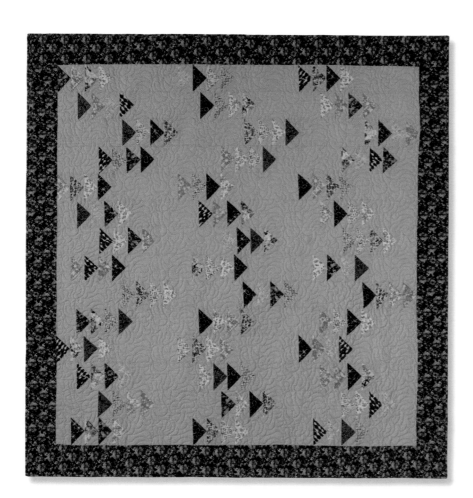

take flight

QUILT SIZE
76½" X 81"

BLOCK SIZE
5" x 10" finished

QUILT TOP
2 packages 5" print squares
3¾ yards background fabric

BORDER
1½ yard

BINDING
¾ yard

BACKING
2 yards 90" wide

SAMPLE QUILT
Indigo Rose by Sara B for Camelot
Fabrics

QUILTING PATTERN
Birds

ONLINE TUTORIALS
msqc.co/blockearlywinter17

PATTERN
pg. 46

two-way street

QUILT SIZE
74" x 86"

BLOCK SIZE
10" finished

SUPPLIES
2 packages of 5" print squares
4¼ yards background fabric
  – includes inner border

OUTER BORDER
1½ yards

BINDING
¾ yard

BACKING
5¼ yards - vertical seam(s)

SAMPLE QUILT
Oak Grove Lane by Kathy Schmitz
for Moda Fabrics

QUILTING PATTERN
Loops & Swirls

ONLINE TUTORIALS
msqc.co/blockearlywinter17

PATTERN
pg. 54

windmill

QUILT SIZE
76" X 92"

BLOCK SIZE
16" finished

QUILT TOP
1 roll 2½" print strips
4½ yards background fabric

BORDER
1½ yards

BINDING
¾ yard

BACKING
5¾ yards - vertical seam(s)

OTHER
MSQC Large Simple Wedge
Template

SAMPLE QUILT
Drizzle by Kathy Engle for Island
Batiks

QUILTING PATTERN
Sticky Buns

ONLINE TUTORIALS
msqc.co/blockearlywinter17

PATTERN
pg. 62

dresden zippered pouch

DRESDEN ZIPPERED POUCH

Finished Size: approximately 8½" x 9"

SUPPLY LIST

(4 - 8) 5" print squares
(1) 5½" x 20" rectangle
(2) 2½" x 20" contrasting strips
(1) 9" x 20" rectangle - lining
(1) 9" x 20" rectangle fusible batting
Nylon zipper
MSQC Dresden Plate Template

ZIPPERED GIFT CARD POUCH

Finished Size: 3½" x 4½"

SUPPLY LIST

4½" x 10½" rectangle
4½" x 10½" rectangle - lining
4½" x 10½" rectangle fusible batting
Nylon zipper

SAMPLE QUILT

Berries and Blossoms from Zentex

ONLINE TUTORIALS

msqc.co/blockearlywinter17

PATTERN

pg. 78

construction basics

general quilting

- All seams are ¼" inch unless directions specify differently.
- Cutting instructions are given at the point when cutting is required.
- Precuts are not prewashed; therefore do not prewash other fabrics in the project.
- All strips are cut width of fabric.
- Remove all selvages.

press seams

- Use a steam iron on the cotton setting.
- Press the seam just as it was sewn right sides together. This "sets" the seam.
- With dark fabric on top, lift the dark fabric and press back.
- The seam allowance is pressed toward the dark side. Some patterns may direct otherwise for certain situations.
- Follow pressing arrows in the diagrams when indicated.
- Press toward borders. Pieced borders may demand otherwise.
- Press diagonal seams open on binding to reduce bulk.

borders

- Always measure the quilt top 3 times before cutting borders.
- Start measuring about 4" in from each side and through the center vertically.
- Take the average of those 3 measurements.
- Cut 2 border strips to that size. Piece strips together if needed.
- Attach one to either side of the quilt.

- Position the border fabric on top as you sew. The feed dogs can act like rufflers. Having the border on top will prevent waviness and keep the quilt straight.
- Repeat this process for the top and bottom borders, measuring the width 3 times.
- Include the newly attached side borders in your measurements.
- Press toward the borders.

binding

find a video tutorial at: www.msqc.co/006

- Use 2½" strips for binding.
- Sew strips end-to-end into one long strip with diagonal seams, aka the plus sign method (next). Press seams open.
- Fold in half lengthwise wrong sides together and press.
- The entire length should equal the outside dimension of the quilt plus 15" - 20."

plus sign method

- Lay one strip across the other as if to make a plus sign right sides together.
- Sew from top inside to bottom outside corners crossing the intersections of fabric as you sew. Trim excess to ¼" seam allowance.
- Press seam open.

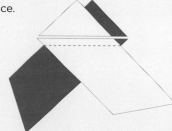

find a video tutorial at: www.msqc.co/001

attach binding

- Match raw edges of folded binding to the quilt top edge.
- Leave a 10" tail at the beginning.
- Use a ¼" seam allowance.
- Start in the middle of a long straight side.

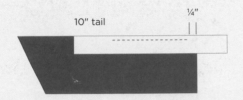

10" tail   ¼"

miter corners

- Stop sewing ¼" before the corner.
- Move the quilt out from under the presser foot.
- Clip the threads.
- Flip the binding up at a 90° angle to the edge just sewn.
- Fold the binding down along the next side to be sewn, aligning raw edges.
- The fold will lie along the edge just completed.
- Begin sewing on the fold.

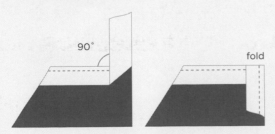

90°   fold

close binding

MSQC recommends The Binding Tool from TQM Products to finish binding perfectly every time.

- Stop sewing when you have 12" left to reach the start.
- Where the binding tails come together, trim excess leaving only 2½" of overlap.
- It helps to pin or clip the quilt together at the two points where the binding starts and stops. This takes the pressure off of the binding tails while you work.
- Use the plus sign method to sew the two binding ends together, except this time when making the plus sign, match the edges. Using a pencil, mark your sewing line because you won't be able to see where the corners intersect. Sew across.

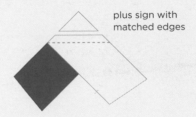

plus sign with matched edges

- Trim off excess; press seam open.
- Fold in half wrong sides together, and align all raw edges to the quilt top.
- Sew this last binding section to the quilt. Press.
- Turn the folded edge of the binding around to the back of the quilt and tack into place with an invisible stitch or machine stitch if you wish.